CHRISTIAN ERROR DEBUNKED!

LINDA HUDSON

Copyright

Dedication

I would like to dedicate this book to the following people in my life:

JESUS – For being the eternal HERO of my Life who will never leave me

CECIL – My husband, an amazing Bible scholar and teacher in the word and the Priest of my home who continues to teach me and wash me in the word.

BRAYDEN – My son, who is an amazing Father and will lead his family to learn of and to follow Jesus!

Table of Contents

AUTHOR's NOTE

In this book I will try to present a pretty simple overview and teaching on some of the misconceptions that we as Christians have believed for so long with NO real evidence based on scripture. I do this because some of these lies keep some people bound under a very oppressive, controlling and legalistic mindset not allowing them to live a new life IN CHRIST that will bring them through it all to VICTORY in JESUS!

I pray that we stop echoing the things we just hear from others and study it for our self...I admonish all of us to open the Holy Bible and DIG DEEPER!

JESUS....IS and always was....MY ANSWER!

INTRODUCTION

After releasing my memoir, "Jilted to Jesus", I felt a need to just "touch on" some things that the Lord has shown me in His Word. I by no means claim to be a Biblical Scholar, and there are so many amazing and brilliant minds and scholars out there that I can recommend. They can go into some very deep theological teachings on the subjects that I only touch on. I have by no means "arrived" spiritually and am continuing to learn and grow in The Word. I do recommend that for any additional teachings or clarification, please study to show yourself approved and look into other teachers' works.

However I did want to share just a few things, even if only at "surface level" that I think some may be able to benefit from. Coming out of certain "legalistic denominations" I have had to study as a Berean and learn some things with the help of my husband, other teachers and the Holy Spirit, as certain denominations, organizations or movements, will only teach you based on their specific agenda or ideology and will not get outside of that thinking. I do find that this "close minded" study approach will typically not search out the complete context in the word from cover to cover.

I also never intend to put a personal spin on what is shared in this book, as I want to stay rooted and ground in the WORD as God wrote it, and never get outside of His teaching. I also NEVER want to go seek man's wisdom in some other pagan or new age thoughts and "steal them back" from the enemy or mix them with The Bible to make them "palatable".

So I hope these few teachings I've shared will bring just a little more clarity and bless you with some freedom.

MY SEARCH FOR TRUTH...

CHAPTER ONE

WOMEN ISSUES

Are women allowed to wear PANTS?

□ □ □

The first time I ever experienced women being oppressed was in a church setting in a very legalistic denomination. We were told that in order for us to BE HOLY, we could NOT wear pants, makeup, and jewelry or cut our hair. When I started to see the horrific hurts and issues this oppressive mindset caused, not only to older women, but the younger women, I began my DIG into the Holy Bible to see what it says. Here is my discovery.

First I had to find out why they believed what they believed. Most in this denomination take the following argument for NOT wearing pants from Deuteronomy 22:5.

First, I commend women for wanting to dress modestly. We Christian women should ALL have this same HEART to do so. I also commend you for standing strong in your "personal" convictions; absolutely we should all have the courage to do that. I would encourage you to abide by YOUR "personal" convictions that align with the Word of God.

I would also suggest that you read the Book of Galatians and others in the New Testament as it is full of the revelation that we have come into a new covenant. Jesus came to bring us this new "WAY" of living, and Jesus constantly battled against the Pharisees who had perfected religion and the law.

When we study the Bible, I challenge us all to PLEASE stop taking one verse out of context and read the Bible cover to cover for its entire revelation, and read it in context of who was talking to who for what purpose, at what time, in what culture, and it helps to read it in the original language it was written.

On that note...I just want to share what this verse in Deuteronomy 22:5 says. We read....Deuteronomy 22:5- *The woman shall not wear that which pertaineth* (means "armor"-Hebrew) *unto a man* (means "warrior"-Hebrew)....If we read this in the original language, it SAYS-"**The woman shall not wear armor that is unto a warrior.**" See how reading it in the Hebrew it reveals the true meaning of the text? In the pagan culture, one form of worship to their false warrior goddess was to put on the armor of a warrior, and stand before her in worship of her (this false goddess)....**THIS** was the **abomination** in which this verse speaks of, NOT "wearing pants".

I believe most Bible teachers teach that when you study the Bible you cannot take ONE verse out of context and you have to read the Bible as a whole, and understand that we lose some meanings of the words from Hebrew to English. For example if we simply look at the word "man" here in Deuteronomy 22:5 it means "warrior", where in Deuteronomy 22:13 the same word "man" means "male"person. This is because the word is meant to convey the different meaning in a text.

When you quote something from the Book of the LAW (Deuteronomy) you have to also consider in that Judaic culture they were still under the old covenant, and they had 613 laws in which to abide by. If we move to the New covenant which Jesus came to bring, we read in (*James 2:10-For whosoever shall keep the whole LAW, and yet offend (not obey it) in one point, he is GUILTY of all*).

If you are going to take ONE LAW out of the Old Testament then you also are required to keep ALL the laws, and we know that there is not one man that is perfect or able to do this, ONLY JESUS, that is why God had to send Jesus....to redeem us from the curse of the law. If we were going to be made holy ONLY by the laws we keep, there would be no need for Jesus to have come, (*Mark 7:13 Making the word of God of none effect through your tradition, which ye have delivered: and many such like things do ye.*) We are NO LONGER under the works of the law, but under the NEW covenant, through faith in Jesus Christ. (***Galatians 3:10** For as many as are of the works of the law are under the curse:*

19

for it is written, Cursed is every one that **continueth NOT in all things which are written in the book of the law** *to do them. 11 But that no man is justified by the law in the sight of God, it is evident: for, The just shall live by faith. 12 And the law is not of faith: but, The man that doeth them shall live in them. 13 Christ hath redeemed us from the curse of the law, being made a curse for us: for it is written, Cursed is every one that hangeth on a tree: 14 That the blessing of Abraham might come on the Gentiles through Jesus Christ; that we might receive the promise of the Spirit through faith.*). **The LAW was our "schoolmaster" UNTIL the seed of the promise (Jesus) came. We are justified (made righteous) by our faith in Christ. (***Galatians 3:23** But before faith came, we were kept under the law, shut up unto the faith which should afterwards be revealed. 24 Wherefore the law was our schoolmaster to* **bring us unto Christ***, that we might be justified by faith. 25 But after that faith is come, we are no longer under a schoolmaster.*). **God does not look at the outside but at our HEART (***1 Samuel 16:7** But the LORD said unto Samuel, Look not on his countenance, or on the height of his stature; because I have refused him: for the LORD seeth not as man seeth; for man looketh on the outward appearance, but the LORD looketh on the* **HEART***.*).

My prayer for all is that you will no longer be under the bondage of the law, and that you will not be FALLEN FROM GRACE...(*Galatians 5:1** Stand fast therefore in the* **liberty wherewith Christ hath made us free***, and be not entangled again with the yoke of bondage. 2 Behold, I Paul say unto you, that if ye be circumcised, Christ shall* *profit you nothing. 3 For I testify again to every man that is circumcised, that he is a debtor to do the whole law.* ***4 Christ is become of no effect unto you, whosoever of you are justified by the law; ye are fallen from grace.****).*

May the Holy Ghost give you an illumination of the Word of God... keep pressing in... we are HIS daughters.

CHAPTER TWO

WOMEN ISSUES

*Are women allowed to wear make-up
or jewelry?*

□   □   □

Continuing along the same line of thought, we then move to another man made rule that women should not wear makeup as this is not considered holy and may even get one accused of being a Jezebel.

The Bible verse that is used to support this teaching is found in…

*1 Timothy 2:9 In like manner also, that women adorn themselves in modest apparel, with **shamefacedness** and sobriety; not with broided hair, or gold, or pearls, or costly array;*

The word "shamefacedness" here some take to mean "Plain face" or "NO MAKEUP". This is NOT what the word means. The word "shamefacedness" actually means in the Greek "downcast eyes and bashfulness, modesty or reverence towards men". In other words…DON'T be FLIRTY with men…which is good advice if you are modest and holy.

Again, let's take the chapter in the whole context as it was written. These were instructions about prayer and the place of women in the church. Back in the day of the Judaic culture, Jewish women had a whole separate section inside the temple service for which their custom said they were to pray (with their heads covered) and they were not to speak in the church, but in Jewish culture, to learn and ask questions of their husband at home. This was according to their culture.

Again we see where the Greek word was used to convey a meaning of godliness, and not "worldliness" …thus also addressing the "broided hair, gold, or pearls, or costly array". This was never meant for you to NOT wear makeup…but take on a holy demeanor in prayer.

Along the same thought process GOD looks at the intents of our heart during our worship and prayer to him… that we did not just come into the church so people could see what we are wearing or how our hair is fixed, or to be flirting with men so as to draw attention to us.

As for wearing of jewelry, why would the Lord say the following to his people in Jerusalem if wearing jewelry was condemned? WHY would GOD put jewelry on his people if it was NOT what HE intended or if he considered it a sin? Isn't he the same yesterday, today and forever?

Ezekiel 16:8-14 *8 Now when I passed by thee, and looked upon thee, behold, thy time was the time of love; and I spread my skirt over thee, and covered thy nakedness: yea, **I sware unto thee, and entered into a covenant with thee, saith the Lord GOD, and thou becamest mine.** 9 Then washed I thee with water; yea, I throughly washed away thy blood from thee, and **I anointed thee with oil.** 10 I clothed thee also with broidered work, and shod thee with badgers' skin, and I girded thee about with fine linen, and I covered thee with silk. 11 **I decked thee also with ornaments, and I put bracelets upon thy hands, and a chain on thy neck.** 12 **And I put a jewel on thy forehead, and earrings in thine ears,** and a beautiful crown upon thine head. 13 Thus wast thou **decked with gold and silver;** and thy raiment was of fine linen, and silk, and broidered work; thou didst eat fine flour, and honey, and oil: and thou wast exceeding beautiful, and thou didst prosper into a kingdom. 14 And thy renown went forth among the heathen for thy beauty: for it was perfect through my comeliness, **which I had put upon thee, saith the Lord GOD.***

Again, I believe these things do not make us holy or unholy...I believe the BLOOD of JESUS makes us righteous and justified, the Word of God continues to sanctify us before HIM. I also believe that he does not want us to lust after these things in our heart, and to not allow the power of coveting these things to overcome us. Paul states this here...

1 Corinthians 6: [11] *And such were some of you: but ye are washed, but ye are sanctified, but ye are justified in the name of the Lord Jesus, and by the Spirit of our God.* [12] ***All things are lawful*** *unto me, but all things are not expedient: all things are lawful for me,* ***but I will not be brought under the power of any.***

So in everything we do for the Lord, I believe that we put HIM first and trust that we are saved by grace through FAITH in Christ Jesus!

CHAPTER THREE

WOMEN ISSUES

Are women allowed to cut their hair?

□ □ □

The next issue I would like for us to examine, is the issue of whether women are "allowed" to cut their hair? Some teach that "hair" is their glory?

This rule is taken from …

1 Corinthians 11:10 For this cause ought the woman to have power on her head because of the angels.

First off just think about the "logic" of this belief and if just having long hair gives you power or glory, then when I was twelve years old and never cut my hair, I should have had holy glory or power…however, I was in the beginning phases of drug addiction. You can read about my "Testimony" in my BOOK "Jilted to Jesus".

Secondly, if just having long hair makes you powerful and full of glory and holiness, what about "prostitutes" in today's culture that actually never cut their hair? Doesn't even make logical sense right?

Third and final point I want to make is to consider who Paul was speaking to and for what purpose. In any letter, it will usually start with an introductory statement and end with a final summary statement.

This Chapter deals with a "cultural" issue of that day, but we don't want to base what we do on culture...however we do want to get the full context of the purpose and meaning of the scriptures. The cultural issues of that day were one concerning the covering of the head in prayer and the length of hair on men and women.

During this time, remember, there were new believers that were coming out of both the Jewish and Pagan religious beliefs. These new believers were now all worshipping together and they were intermingling some of their old ways, traditions and practices. There was a lot of confusion in the worship services because of this.

In the Jewish culture, men were required to wear a *kippah,* a small round cap to be upon the head of all devout Jews on the Sabbath and any time the Torah was read or prayers went up. Jewish women were also required to worship separate from the men, and they were considered women of honor by the veil (covering) they would wear in public. If they did not wear the veil, women were considered to be a harlot. In the Temple of old, the females occupied, according to Jewish tradition, a

27

raised gallery along three sides of the court. They were allowed to observe the ceremonies but never to participate in them. Rabbinic literature was filled with contempt for women. The rabbis taught that women were not to be saluted, or spoken to in the street, and they were not to be instructed in the law or receive an inheritance. A woman walked six paces behind her husband.

Also among the Gentiles if a woman was guilty of adultery, or if she was a common slave, or prostitute, her head was shaved. At Corinth, there were also pagan priestesses who "pretended" to give oracles from the gods and did so with their head uncovered.

With so many *new* female converts, Paul again as stated in his summary verse, was trying to **bring order** into this crazy mingled and mangled mess of a worship service. He instructs them to pray with a "covering", a veil on their heads to ensure that believers did not confuse the true Godly women with pagans inside the church.

This confusion and disorder in the Corinthian church was causing division and there were some that were even bringing false teachings or heresies into the new believers.

So with a little bit of cultural history, we can now read 1 Corinthians 11 maybe with some more clarity.

Let us look at what Paul says in his "introductory statement" in the first two verses of 1 Corinthians 11…

*1 Corinthians 11:1 Be ye **followers** of me, even as I also am **of Christ**. ²Now I praise you, brethren, that ye remember me in all things, and **keep the ordinances, as I delivered them to you.***

And let us now look at his "summary statement"...

*1 Corinthians 11: ³⁴And if any man hunger, let him eat at home; that ye come not together unto condemnation. And **the rest will I set in order when I come**.*

Let's continue to see what the Bible has to say in 1 Corinthians 11. We will take the whole chapter into context of what Paul was actually trying to communicate. We will also look at the original meanings of the words in GREEK that will give us a better idea of what Paul is also saying.

*1 Corinthians 11:1 Be ye followers of me, even as I also am of Christ. ²Now I praise you, brethren, that ye remember me in all things, and **keep the ordinances**, as I delivered them to you.*

Paul's introducing his purpose...to get them back to the original ordinances and teachings he had already brought them.

1 Corinthians 11:3 But I would have you know, that the head of every man is Christ; and the head of the woman is the man; and the head of Christ is God.

This states an order of creation to remind us that Christ is our supreme authority…all authority flows from Him.

1 Corinthians 11:⁴ Every man praying or prophesying, having his head covered, dishonoureth his head.

Again, a Jewish custom for a man to wear his *kippah* when praying or reading the Torah.

1 Corinthians 11:⁵ But every woman that prayeth or prophesieth with her head uncovered dishonoureth her head: for that is even all one as if she were shaven.

As stated previously, if women were participating in worship services not having her head covered, she would end up dishonoring not only her husband, but Christ. Paul states here if she does not wear a covering, she will be confused with or considered as a woman who was shaven (a harlot or pagan).

1 Corinthians 11:⁶ For if the woman be not covered, let her also be shorn: but if it be a shame for a woman to be shorn or shaven, let her be covered.

Paul was stating that in order to bring an end to the confusion, he states that if she refused to wear a covering she should just go ahead and shave her head (as a harlot or pagan), but he reminds Godly women in order to not bring shame upon themselves, which will also bring shame on their husbands, they should wear a veil.

1 Corinthians 11:⁷ For a man indeed ought not to cover his head, forasmuch as he is the image and glory of God: but the woman is the glory of the man.

Paul states that really since a man is covered by Christ that maybe he should just leave his head uncovered, but he again states that a woman is to bring honor to her husband.

1 Corinthians 11:⁸ For the man is not of the woman: but the woman of the man.

Paul reminds us here that man was not created by the woman (but God), but the woman was taken from the man (his side) during creation.

1 Corinthians 11:⁹ Neither was the man created for the woman; but the woman for the man.

Paul reminds us here the reason God created the woman…was man needed a helpmeet.

¹⁰ For this cause ought the woman to have power on her head because of the angels.

Paul says for this reason, the woman shall have power (authority, privilege and freedom) because of the angels (messengers… that were sent to deliver this message of freedom in Christ).

*1 Corinthians 11:[11] Nevertheless neither is the man without the woman, neither the woman without the man, in the Lord. [12] For as the woman is of the man, even so is the man also by the woman; but **all things of God**.*

Paul I believe is repeating a thought taken from Galatians 3:28 which states …"there is neither male nor female: for ye **are all one** in Christ Jesus".

1 Corinthians 11:[13] Judge in yourselves: is it comely that a woman pray unto God uncovered?

Very important to note that Paul is telling them to "judge in or among themselves", and asks the question "is it comely (suitable or proper) that a woman pray unto God uncovered"?

1 Corinthians 11:[14] Doth not even nature itself teach you, that, if a man have long hair, it is a shame unto him?

Paul says to look at the natural world (secular) there were also male prostitutes in the pagan temples that did not cut their hair and were effeminate. Paul suggests for men to cut their hair as to not confuse believers, again to bring order to their worship services.

1 Corinthians 11:[15] But if a woman have long hair, it is a glory to her: for her hair is given her for a covering.

Paul reiterates that a woman that had long hair in their current culture was considered to be a woman of glory (dignity, honor)—not a harlot or pagan, as her hair is her natural covering (veil).

*1 Corinthians 11:¹⁶ But if any man seem to be contentious, **we have no such custom**, neither the churches of God.*

Here is a **KEY POINT**, Paul states that if ANY man seems to be contentious (has a quarrel, strife or dispute) with this; he says that we have NO SUCH **custom** (usage).

1 Corinthians 11:¹⁷ Now in this that I declare unto you I praise you not, that ye come together not for the better, but for the worse.

Paul rebuked them that he would NOT praise them because when they were coming together they were not getting better, but worse.

1 Corinthians 11:¹⁸ For first of all, when ye come together in the church, I hear that there be divisions among you; and I partly believe it.

He said he has heard that in the church there were divisions among them, and he believed it (because of what he saw).

33

*1 Corinthians 11:¹⁹ For there must be also **heresies among you**, that they which are approved may be made manifest among you.*

He pointed out that there must be heresies that were approved and brought in among them.

1 Corinthians 11:²⁰ When ye come together therefore into one place, this is not to eat the Lord's supper.²¹ For in eating every one taketh before other his own supper: and one is hungry, and another is drunken.²² What? have ye not houses to eat and to drink in? or despise ye the church of God, and shame them that have not? what shall I say to you? Shall I praise you in this? I praise you not.

Paul rebuked them and told them they were not to come in to this gathering of worship to eat, and drink the Lord 's Supper, or to get drunk. He asked, "Don't you have houses that you can eat and drink in?" He rebuked them and asked if they despised the church of God? He told them he would NOT praise them for their paganistic behavior!

1 Corinthians 11:²³ For I have received of the Lord that which also I delivered unto you, that the Lord Jesus the same night in which he was betrayed took bread:²⁴ And when he had given thanks, he brake it, and said, Take, eat: this is my body, which is broken for you: this do in remembrance of me.²⁵ After the same manner also he took the cup, when he had supped, saying, this cup is the new testament in my blood: this do ye, as oft as ye drink it, in remembrance of me.²⁶ For as often as ye eat *this bread, and drink this cup, ye do shew the Lord's death till he come.²⁷ Wherefore whosoever shall eat this bread, and drink this cup of the Lord, unworthily, shall be guilty of the body and blood of the Lord.*

Paul brought to their attention what Jesus had taught them to do in remembrance of Him by practicing communion.

1 Corinthians 11:²⁸ But let a man examine himself, and so let him eat of that bread, and drink of that cup.²⁹ For he that eateth and drinketh unworthily, eateth and drinketh damnation to himself, not discerning the Lord's body .³⁰ For this cause many are weak and sickly among you, and many sleep.

Paul suggested that we do not practice communion without first examining our heart, and that we do not eat or drink unworthily as we may bring on damnation to ourselves…he even said this may be the cause that many were weak or sick or dying.

1 Corinthians 11:³¹ For if we would judge ourselves, we should not be judged.³² But when we are judged, we are chastened of the Lord, that we should not be condemned with the world.

He said to again judge our own heart, so the Lord doesn't judge and send His chastening.

1 Corinthians 11:[33] *Wherefore, my brethren, when ye come together to eat, tarry one for another.*[34] *And if any man hunger, let him eat at home; that ye come not together unto condemnation. And the* **rest will I set in order when I come.**

Paul states here that when we come together to eat to tarry one for another. He says eat at home before you come together to avoid condemnation.

THEN Paul states "the rest will **I SET IN ORDER** when I come"!! He was simply bringing order to the church.

So I hope this helps make this issue of "NOT CUTTING YOUR HAIR" clear. We have to learn to NOT take one verse in a whole chapter out of context.

God looks at our "heart" and we are not judged "holy" by what is on the outside, like the Pharisee's robes.

CHAPTER FOUR

WOMEN ISSUES

*Are Women Allowed to Preach or
Speak in the Church?*

□   □   □

This topic is always a very "controversial" topic, and has been debated to death. So, I am not here to debate, but hope to bring a little clarity to the issue.

Scripture must always be studied and viewed as a whole within the complete context. We cannot not take one verse out of context and use it to fit our own religious or personal narrative. It also cannot be used to cancel out other scriptures. So many great Bible teachers are seeing scripture through a mindset of what they have been taught and listened to all their life, their traditions, and this produces a "biased" opinion of the word.

When we read the Bible we also need to "see through" the male chauvinistic view of a culture in which it was written. We will need to study and research the culture in order to determine what the new Christians

37

were led to believe about women based on the infiltration of a Greek, Roman and Jewish mindset. They had intermingled the teachings of the world within their everyday thinking which affected their actions.

The Jews allowed the Greek and Roman culture to bias their thoughts of women, and viewed them closer to slaves, possessions or simply sexual beings. The Pharisees even tried to avoid looking at or talking to women. Jewish women were marginalized in worship services. The architects of Herod's temple went so far as to build actual walls that divided people. There were separate courts that divided Jews from Gentiles, and Jewish men from Jewish women.

By the time Jesus came along in the second century, archaeology suggest that the synagogues kept women in screened in second floor galleries that they entered by a back door. The rabbis also decreed that a synagogue could only be established wherever there was a quorum of ten **men** (not women), and this is not in scripture. Women were excluded from a public reading of the Torah, and they said that women reading the Torah would dishonor it. Women were also discouraged from private study of the Torah, and their laws encouraged them to learn from their husband at home.

There was a Jew named Philo of Alexandria who chose to MIX the writings of Moses and a Greek philosopher, Aristotle, which is only the "reasoning of man"...not God's TRUTH. This dangerous thinking of Greek philosophy would spread and infect more religious teachings even through all Western civilization. Greek philosophies were built on the idea that "man" is the measure of all things, and that using his own "reasoning ability" he can figure all things out. The Bible teaches that man's wisdom (finite) is foolishness to God, and that God (infinite) created humanity. The Bible also teaches us that God's ways are not our ways; HIS thoughts are NOT our thoughts! How can the "finite" man's mind even begin to comprehend the "infinite" mind of God? Philo tried to combine the finite "rational" thoughts of the Greeks, with the "infinite" revealed TRUTH of the Bible. Philo also loved Greek culture, and assuming what he wrote adopted the Greek's contempt for women. He stated firmly that "the male is more perfect than the female", and other things he wrote demeaning women.

Josephus, a Jewish historian also tried to combine Judaism with the cultural philosophy of his time. So did Sirach, a writer of the Apocrypha, who blamed the fall all on Eve, instead of the shared responsibility also on Adam.

So with a little background I say we now look at some scriptures. First I want to address the man shall "rule" over women issue. Let's start in the first three Chapters of Genesis. I will only address the male female issues in these Chapters, not the order of Creation.

Genesis 1:26 And God said, Let us make man (mankind) in our image, after our likeness: and let THEM *have dominion OVER the fish of the sea, and over the fowl of the air, and over the cattle, and over ALL the EARTH, and over every creeping think that creepeth upon the earth. 27 So God created man (mankind) in his own image, in the image of God created he him (mankind): MALE and FEMALE created he **THEM**! 28 And God blessed **THEM**, and God said unto **THEM**, Be **fruitful** and **multiply**, and **replenish** the earth, and **subdue it**: and **have dominion** over the **fish** of the sea, and over the **fowl** of the air, and over every **living thing** that moveth upon the earth. 31 And God saw EVERY thing that HE had made, and, behold, it was VERY GOOD. And the evening and the morning were the sixth day.*

So we see here in verse 26 they were given dominion over all the earth and in verse 27 that GOD made the woman in his image along with the man. God **never** GAVE the man only dominion or rule over the woman here. We also see in verse 28 God blessed the man along with the woman and said unto them to be fruitful and multiply and replenish the earth, and subdue it and have dominion over the fish and every living thing that moves on the earth. God then saw and declared everything He made was **very good** in verse 31.

In Genesis 2:7-17 we see where God FORMED the male person from the dust of the ground, and put him in a garden eastward in Eden. In verse 15 we see the males purpose in the garden of Eden was to "dress" (work) it and to "keep" (guard) it. In verse 16 we see the Lord COMMANDED the MALE person ONLY, as the woman

40

was not made here yet. God commanded the male to eat freely from every tree of the garden, yet the tree of KNOWLEDGE of good and evil, he shall NOT eat, for he would surely die.

Then in Genesis 2:22 the Lord God took a rib from Adam and made the woman. Then God spoke a command in verse 24 that a man shall leave his father and his mother and shall cleave unto his wife: and they shall be one flesh.

Then we come to Genesis 3 where the snake was subtle and he said unto the woman, "Yea, hath GOD SAID, Ye shall not eat of every tree of the garden?". We also see where the woman misquoted the mandate give to Adam in verse 3 because she added "neither shall ye touch it". So who was not communicating with her the COMPLETE words of the Lord command? Her husband? Then the serpent lied and told her in verses 4 and 5 that she would not die but that her eyes (of **enlightenment**) would be opened and she **shall be as gods** (*plural*), knowing good and evil. So the woman ate the fruit and gave also unto her husband (Adam) **who was with her** in verse 6, and they BOTH ATE. Shared responsibility for "the fall".

After the fall, God issued a couple of curses and consequences for their disobedience. In Genesis 3:14 God said to the serpent..."thou art cursed", and God said

41

in verse 17 "cursed is the ground". However I do not read where he cursed the woman or Adam. Instead he issued consequences of her sin to the woman in verse 16 he said *"I will greatly multiply thy sorrow and thy conception; in sorrow thou shalt bring forth children; and thy desire shall be to thy husband, and **HE** shall **RULE OVER THEE** ".* So we see here this "ruling over a woman by the man" was a result of sin, **AFTER the fall**. So if God has redeemed us back to the original place of NO SIN, should we still be under a consequence of SIN? NO!

We also see that another consequence for disobedience was given to Adam in verse 17, God said, *"Because thou hast hearkened unto the voice of thy wife, and hast eaten of the tree, of which **I commanded THEE**, saying **Thou shalt not eat of it**: cursed is the ground for **thy sake;** in sorrow shat thou eat of it all the days of thy life; (v.18) Thorns also and thistles shall it bring forth to thee; and thou shalt eat the herb of the field; (v. 19) In the sweat of thy face shalt thou eat bread, till thou return unto the ground; for out of it wast thou taken; for dust thou art, and unto dust shalt thou return".* So God here promised Adam he would work hard just to eat all the days of his life, and his provision would come from the thing he was made of, the earth…dirt. God NEVER cursed Adam or the woman, just the serpent and the ground. They were given hard consequences AFTER the Fall, which entailed living on a "cursed earth" with a "cursed enemy".

We move into a NEW Covenant with Jesus, and you can read where Jesus came to completely destroy tradition. Mary would sit at his feet to learn from this amazing teacher/rabbi, and this was unheard of because women never were allowed to do this. Jesus would speak to a Samaritan woman at the well and after her salvation; she would go preach to her city, "Come see a man...". So many examples in the New Testament even of where the Apostle Paul would have women with him that labored with him in the Gospel. There would be Phoebe a deacon in the church at Cenchrea, who Paul entrusted his letter to the Romans for her to deliver for him. Priscilla who worked with Aquila her husband to "educate" Apollos. Philip the evangelist had four virgin daughters who prophesied in Acts 21:9. And then the Apostle Junia, who was greeted by Paul as "outstanding among the apostles" in Romans 16:7, was a woman. In Revelation 2:20-24 Christ rebuke the Thyatiran church for allowing a **false** prophetess called "Jezebel" to teach. If it was a crime for women to teach the brethren, why wouldn't the Lord rebuke this church for allowing a woman to teach instead of singling out just the "false" teaching?

As we move into some of the Pastoral epistles, we come to: 1 Timothy 2:11 which says, "Let the woman learn in silence (*hesuchia*[quietness]) with all subjection" (v.12)"But I suffer (permit) not a woman to teach, nor to usurp authority over the man, but to be in silence (*hesuchia*[quietness]). We will examine this Chapter which gives instructions for prayer for men and women in the church. If we move back up to verse 2 we see "all believers" are to lead a "quiet" and peaceable life in all godliness and honesty. Silence is the same word, "quiet". Paul was constantly bringing order and peace to the churches, and in the church of Ephesus, there were people promoting false teaching, worshipping Artemis. The church of Corinth was out of order with everyone praying, prophesying and speaking in tongues all at the same time, drinking the communion wine, eating the communion bread…no order.

We read in 1 Thessalonians 4:11 Pauls instructs ALL believers to "strive eagerly to be quiet, to do your own business and work with your own hands". Quietness, peaceable life and church order is a prerequisite for the saint's lifestyle.

Since 1 Timothy 2:11 and 12 was directed to a woman (singular), and not women (plural) like in verse 10, I believe he was specifically instructing one (singular) woman who was out of order. Verse 11 says "Let the woman (singular) learn in silence with all subjection", which was a law of their custom and culture that women were to learn at home from their husbands. Verse 12 states "But I suffer (permit) NOT a woman (singular) to teach, nor to usurp authority over the man, but to be in silence". I believe Paul was rebuking one woman for not abiding in the custom.

Again as in Judaic custom, women were to remain silent in their synagogue and not allowed to read from the Torah much less teach, and had their own separate section from the men. You cannot read this verse without reading it within the context of their culture. The reason is that today in church services, we have women that are included and not separated from the men...so we are obviously living in a different day and culture.

It's also interesting as a side note that in verse 14 it says "And Adam was not deceived, but the woman being deceived was in the transgression"?? In Paul's rebuke of this one woman, was he reminding her of the order of "creation" in verses 13-15 to keep her in line? Re-read Genesis...Adam was the one that God commanded to NOT eat of the tree...not the woman...and Adam was right there with her, so BOTH Adam and Eve share in the responsibility of the sin of eating from the tree of knowledge of good and evil. Yikes! It is also noted in verse 8 that men should pray "without wrath and doubting" so again, Paul is bringing order to the church even for men.

I would like to also clarify that in verse 9 women should adorn themselves in modest apparel (not low cut or sexually provoking dress). The word shamefacedness here also does NOT mean do not wear makeup, but translates out "downcast eyes" and "bashfulness towards men"...so don't be a "flirty girl", no promiscuous clothing or behavior. Also, it is stated here to not even wear your hair jewelry or costly clothing that will draw attention to you...as this can also be considered "not modest".

45

I hope this may bring a little more clarity to the Chapter of 1 Timothy 2.

Now I would like to move on to 1 Corinthians 14:33-35. For the particular issue I would like to look at these few debated versus again about women being in silence in the church. I do recommend you read the whole Chapter of 1 Corinthians 14 as there is a lot in verses 1-22 that expound on spiritual gifts. In verses 23-40 again Paul is bringing order to the Church of Corinth, as he was trying to regulate the use of the spiritual gifts for the church service.

First again, a little more background on the City of Corinth and what Paul was battling against with new believers. This was a large city in Greece that had grown to about 100,000 in total population by the second century. Corinth was a very wealthy city. The city was both a center of arts and culture. It was a city famous for it's promiscuous sexual activity. This city was filled with drunkenness that even their Greek plays were depicted on stage as drunk. Corinth was a port city and known for it's sex trade. They worshiped Aphrodite a Greek goddess of erotic love (Romans called her Venus). The temple of Aphrodite was so wealthy and owned more than a thousand temple-slaves, prostitutes, both men (long hair-effeminate) and women who were dedicated to this goddess. These were "sacred" prostitutes, although there were thousands more "secular" prostitutes. These women added their prayers to the prayers of the city to Aphrodite. This city had a lot of mystery and religious cults. In the secret cult of Dionysus, women would spend days in the high places on the mountains, partying, drinking, revelry, and engaging in sexual immorality. They were known as *maenads* or the crazy mad ones. They boasted of their **enlightment**, altered state of consciousness as a gift from their god of wine and madness.

We have Paul show up on the scene during the year A.D. 50 where he lived with Aquila and Priscilla and was later joined by Silas and Timothy. They preached the gospel of Christ and among this crowd of new believers there were both Jews and Gentiles, slave and free, men and women of all different types of upbringing.

So as we will begin to read Paul's instruction to the church of Corinth, we will first look at his summary statement of this last Chapter in 1 Corinthians 14, verse 40 says, "Let **all things** be **done** decently and **in ORDER**". So again Paul's agenda is to get this church back into a peaceable, quiet order of their worship service.

I will not address the whole Chapter of 14 as I specifically want to teach on the issue of "women" being instructed to not teach in the church.

Let us look at the verses here…

1 Corinthians 14: [23] *If therefore the whole church be come together into one place, and all speak with tongues,* *and there come in those that are **unlearned, or unbelievers**, will they not say that ye are mad?²⁴ But if all prophesy, and there come in one that **believeth not**, or one **unlearned**, he is convinced of all, he is judged of all:²⁵ And thus are the secrets of his heart made manifest; and so falling down on his face he will worship God, and report that God is in you of a truth.*

In verses 23-25 Paul is reminding them here that the goal is to reach "unlearned and unbelievers". That if they come in and everyone is speaking in tongues all at once, the confusion will create fear and the unbeliever will think you are all crazy. He says but if you prophesy a true word from the Lord, it will bring conviction to the unbeliever and the "secrets of his heart" will be made known to him as he will "fall down on his face" in repentance and worship God as he believes in truth.

*1 Corinthians 14: ²⁶ How is it then, brethren? when ye come together, **every one** of you **hath** a psalm, hath a **doctrine**, **hath** a **tongue**, hath a **revelation**, hath an **interpretation**. **Let all things be done unto edifying.**²⁷ If any man speak in an unknown tongue, let it be by two, or at the most by three, and that by course; and let one interpret.²⁸ But if there be no interpreter, let him **keep silence** in the church; and **let him speak to himself, and to God.**²⁹ Let the prophets speak two or three, and let the other judge.³⁰ If any thing be revealed to another that sitteth by, let the first hold his peace.³¹ For **ye may all prophesy one by one**, that all may **learn**, and all may be comforted.³² And the spirits of the prophets are subject to*

the prophets.[33] ***For God is not the author of confusion,
but of peace, as in all churches of the saints.***

Paul was rebuking them as when they were all
coming together they were causing confusion because
everyone was all praying in tongues, interpreting, had a
doctrine, a **revelation**, and this was madness, mass
confusion in their worship services (similar to pagan
practices). He reminds them here that if they cannot bring
an interpretation to their tongues to edify the unbeliever to
be silent…but also states that the one **praying in tongues**
also **speaks to himself and to God**. Why did Paul say he
"speaks to God"? This was a reference to tongues as a
personal prayer language. He says you may all prophesy
in order for the unbeliever to learn and be comforted, and
that the spirit speaking through the prophet is not "out of
control" but is subject to the prophet. Paul finally sums
up this part with "God is **NOT the author of confusion**
but of **peace,** as should be in ALL churches. So in a
church service if it is out of control and brings confusion
and provokes the unbelievers to think your mad or
crazy…DON'T DO IT!

1 Corinthians 14: [34] *Let your women keep **silence** in
the churches: for it is not permitted unto them to speak;
but they are commanded to be under obedience as also
saith the law.*[35] *And if they will learn any thing, let them
ask their husbands at home: for it is a shame for women
to speak in the church.*

In 1 Corinthians 14 verses 34 and 35 we read where Paul is again bringing order out of confusion in this service and states the Judaic law for women to keep silence (quiet) in the church, again to bring a quietness and peaceable service. He also advised them to learn at home from their husbands for it was a shame in Judaic culture for women to publically read from the Torah. Why in this Christian service, did Paul remind them of this law, when they were new believers in Christ? The same reason he was speaking in this whole chapter on other issues of tongues and prophesying...to BRING ORDER to the church service. Greeks and Romans considered women as less than human, slaves or property in the eyes of their culture, and it is my personal belief Paul may have said this for their own protection.

1 Corinthians 14: [36] What? came the word of God out from you? or came it unto you only? [37] If any man think himself to be a prophet, or spiritual, let him acknowledge that the things that I write unto you are the **commandments of the Lord.** *[38] But if any man be ignorant, let him be ignorant. [39] Wherefore, brethren, covet to prophesy, and* **forbid not to speak with tongues.**

Paul summarized this chapter here for the "spiritual" to acknowledge the things he wrote as commandments of the Lord and in continuance of this Paul said in verse 39 **"FORBID NOT to speak with tongues".** Pretty interesting to note this for future reference.

[40] Let all things be done decently and in order

Again, we see where Paul summarized the completion of this letter by saying let ALL things be done decently and IN ORDER!! This was his agenda for this letter.

CHAPTER FIVE

TO JUDGE OR NOT TO JUDGE?

Is Judging Others a Bad Thing?

□□□

To all my brother's and sister's **in Christ**, I first want to preface this teaching by saying...I love you and truly believe that you have SOOO much VALUE to GOD as an adopted son or daughter of God. He sent HIS only son because of the LOVE HE has for you and me, so that we do not have to "stay stuck" in our sin and bondage, as we were sinners in need of a Savior and JESUS came to MAKE us FREE!!! I also know that we are all in our own timetable of transformation and sanctification... however...please let us not become complacent about where we are and where GOD wants us to be...by using excuses and trying to justify this place of compromise. If we truly LOVE and KNOW HIM, we will OBEY HIS commands....it doesn't mean we are perfect...it just means we want ALL that HE has for us!

I wanted to address what I hear SO MANY TIMES coming from "Christian's" that say..."Don't judge me, God doesn't want us to judge"...and then they throw out a "PARTIAL SCRIPTURE" taken out of context of the whole chapter or what the rest of the meaning is. So today…I want us to DIG IN to the scriptures and look for the COMPLETE and WHOLE meaning of what is being communicated!

If we can…let's look at first WHO the "righteous JUDGE" is…

*2 Timothy 4:8-Henceforth there is laid up for me a crown of righteousness, which **the Lord, the righteous judge,** shall give me at that day: and not to me only, but unto all them also that love his appearing.*

There is only ONE RIGHTEOUS JUDGE and that is the Lord. But there will be a JUDGE we face at the end of our lives. Jesus is full of grace and truth (John 1:14), and judges with right judgment (1John 4:8).

In that…God has given us not only HIS WORD to live by and obey, has put HIS HOLY SPIRIT within us to "quicken"(bring to life) our mortal body and bring us conviction to keep us on the right path, but has also equipped and called us to hold each other accountable (submit to one another in the fear of the Lord). HIS word will be used to bring reproof, rebuke and correction when needed, but in love, gentleness, and humility. I am grateful for all the leaders, elders and brethren HE has put in my life to help me see my own blind spots of where I have gotten off track, and have not been walking soberly with HIM.

The scripture I hear most quoted in the "DO NOT JUDGE ME" mantra, comes from... **Matthew 7:1**-- "Do not judge so that you will not be judged. If we stop right there...it really looks like...we should NOT JUDGE. However, let us read on to complete the whole "context"...

Matthew 7: [2] *"For in the WAY you judge, you will be judged; and by your standard of measure, it will be measured to you.* [3] *"Why do you look at the speck that is in your brother's eye, but do NOT notice the log that is in your own eye?* [4] *"Or how can you say to your brother, 'Let me take the speck out of your eye,' and behold, the log is in your own eye?* [5] *"You hypocrite,* **FIRST** *take the log out of your own eye, and* **THEN** *you will* **see clearly** *to* **take the speck out of your brother's eye.***

I don't believe we are to JUDGE with a HYPOCRITAL PIOUS JUDGEMENT, but we are to judge the brethren with a RIGHTEOUS judgment...NOT SELF-RIGTEOUS!

So the context is pointing out what JESUS always hated....PRIDE....self-righteous hypocrites that do not humble themselves first...and think that they are ABOVE others..that have a spirit of religious piety that think they are not equal to others because of their educational degrees, titles, royal robes and membership to their religious organizations of Saducess and Pharisess, and they have put themselves on a very HIGH pedestal or even physical platform.

I do believe Jesus gives us each other and gives GIFTS to HIS BODY for the process of transforming the way we think and becoming more so like HIS IMAGE...not the image of man's righteousness. These scriptures do say **FIRST** take the log out of your own eye, and **THEN** you will see clearly to **TAKE THE SPECK OUT OF YOUR BROTHER's EYE! So...it doesn't say...DON'T EVER JUDGE??**

I believe when we teach and or correct as a leader, we always have to examine our own heart first—and continue to constantly die to ourselves daily!! Die to the need to be "like God"...high and lifted up! I want to continue to move into a place of self-growth, sanctification and walking in holiness and righteousness so that I can become a WITNESS of the GOODNESS of GOD!

In continuance of this thought...that we are to look at our brethren and see where they are STUCK in bondage...let us take a look at the next few chapters, where Paul is bringing correction again to the Church at Corinth.

1 Corinthians 5: [1] *It is reported commonly that there is fornication among you, and such fornication as is not so much as named among the Gentiles, that one should have his father's wife.* [2] *And ye are puffed up, and **have not rather mourned**, that he that hath done this deed* *might be taken away from among you.* *3 For I verily, as absent in body, but present in spirit,* **have judged already,** *as though I were present,* **concerning him that hath so done this deed,** *4 In the name of our Lord Jesus Christ, when ye are gathered together, and my spirit, with the power of our Lord Jesus Christ, 5 To deliver such an one unto Satan for the destruction of the flesh, that the spirit may be saved in the day of the Lord Jesus.6Your glorying is not good. Know ye not that a little leaven leaveneth the whole lump? 7* **Purge out therefore the old leaven,** *that ye may* **be a new lump,** *as ye are unleavened. For even Christ our passover is sacrificed for us: 8 Therefore let us keep the feast, not with old leaven, neither with the leaven of malice and wickedness; but with the unleavened* bread *of sincerity and truth.9* **I wrote unto you in an epistle not to company with fornicators: 10 Yet not altogether with the fornicators of this world, or with the covetous, or extortioners, or with idolaters; for then must ye needs go out of the world.** *11 But now I have written unto you* **not to keep company, if any man that is called a brother be a fornicator,** *or covetous, or an idolater, or a railer, or a* **drunkard,** *or an extortioner;* **with such an one no not to eat.** *12 For* **what have I to do to judge them also that are without? do not ye judge them that are within? 13 But them that are without God judgeth.** *Therefore put away from among yourselves that wicked person.*

Here I have highlighted some parts of this Chapter that I want you to see. The Apostle Paul was writing this to the Corinthians at the close of his three year residence in Ephesus. Paul was bringing correction of error brought

56

about by the carnality of believers at Corinth, they were in an immoral condition. First Paul had to **JUDGE their condition in order to bring the gentle correction needed.** There was a man that slept with his father's wife, and they were compromising and he accused them of being proud and not mourning over this sin among them, and had allowed the man doing this to not be corrected or "taken away from among them". He reminded them that this can affect the whole body…just like leaven (yeast). He reminds them they "become who they associate with" (not to keep company with fornicators among brethren). He reminds them of a previous letter he wrote that they will be in the company of fornicators of this world, or with covetous, or extortioners, or with idolaters, because they cannot go out of the world. But he reminds them that if **any man that is called a brother**, (Christian in your church) **be a fornicator, coveteous, idolater, railer, drunkard, or an extortioner, with SUCH AN ONE, NO NOT TO EAT!** He also says God will judge those that are without (on the outside of the brethren in the world), but asks the question, **do not ye JUDGE them that are within??**

So we see here that a LEADER is correcting the CHURCH to hold the BRETHREN accountable within themselves…and not to become complacent to the sin among the body of Christ.

If we DO NOT say anything to our brother's or sister's about where they are "STUCK' in their SIN—we become "INDIFFERENT" and I would have to beg the question...is this really LOVING THEM?? Or is this enabling them to continue in their bondage because of our lack of courage and fear of gentle confrontation—which is a selfish motive for not confronting?   IS the OPPOSITE of LOVE….."INDIFFERENCE"??

Or….can love grow with the right amount of gentle correction…and allow these brethren to become ALL that GOD intended??

We see Paul continuing this subject...as you can even hear maybe his complete frustration with them going to law against each other in 1 Corinthians 6…

1 Corinthians 6:1-8 [1] *Dare any of you, having a matter against another, go to law before the unjust, and not before the saints?* [2] *Do ye not know that the saints shall judge the world? and if the world shall be judged by you,* **are ye unworthy to judge the smallest matters?** [3] *Know ye not that **we shall judge angels? how much more things that pertain to this life?*** [4] ***If then ye have judgments of things pertaining to this life, set them to judge who are least esteemed in the church.*** [5] *I speak to your shame. Is it so, that there **is not a wise man among you? no, not one that shall be able to judge between his brethren?*** [6] *But brother goeth to law with brother, and that before the unbelievers.* [7] *Now therefore there is utterly a fault among you, because ye go to law one with another. Why do ye not rather take wrong? why do ye not rather* *suffer yourselves to be defrauded? [8] Nay, ye do wrong, and defraud, and that* your *brethren.*

We see here where Paul is asking them in regards to this particular issue , "are ye unworthy to judge the smallest matters?". He reminds them that "we shall judge angels…and asks again if there "is not a wise man among you? No, not one that shall be able to **JUDGE** between his **BRETHREN**?

So in these two chapters…we see where "holding the BODY of Christ, the brethren accountable amongst themselves…is RECOMMENDED by the Apostle Paul himself! Paul is correcting them for **NOT JUDGING amongst themselves those caught in sin.**

*Galatians 6: [1]Brethren, if a man be overtaken in a fault, **ye which are spiritual, restore such an one in the spirit of meekness**; considering thyself, lest thou also be tempted.*

We are to help RESTORE in the spirit of **meekness (gentleness and humility).** We can only RESTORE and bring correction if we look and judge where a person is struggling within their life.

We again…are to NOT have this self-righteous judgment, and we are definitely NOT to JUDGE by APPEARANCES, by what is on the OUTSIDE.

*John 7:24 Judge not according to the appearance, but **judge righteous judgment**.*

Let us be slow to pronounce guilt based on hearsay...and let us presume innocence until sufficient evidence can prove guilt beyond reasonable doubt. Let the goal be restoration (2 Corinthians 13:11). We must be kind to one another, tenderhearted, forgiving one another, as God in Christ forgave us (Ephesians 4:32). Let us follow the Bible's model for church discipline (Matthew 18:15-22).

But I do believe we are called to help bring spiritual RESTORATION to our brother's and sisters in Christ by speaking LIFE and TRUTH into their lives...righteous judgement.

THIS.......IS........COURAGEOUS...........LOVE!!

CHAPTER SIX

GENERATIONAL CURSES

Can Christians Be Cursed?

☐ ☐ ☐

The teaching of "Generational Curses" has been taught mainly by those who have taken on the role of ministers of "deliverance". This teaching, as most, have been taken "out of context" as one verse, instead of the complete. We as believers now live under a new covenant "grace", but even under the old covenant, "the law" we find where God spoke to the nation of Israel as a whole on some issues. Let us just read what the Lord God says about it....

Exodus20:3-6 ³ Thou shalt have no other gods before me. ⁴ Thou shalt not make unto thee any graven image, or any likeness of any thing that is in heaven above, or that is in the earth beneath, or that is in the water under the earth. ⁵ Thou shalt not bow down thyself to them, nor serve them: for I the LORD *thy God am a jealous God, visiting the iniquity of the fathers upon the children unto the third and fourth generation of them that hate me;* ⁶ *And **shewing mercy unto thousands of them that love me, and keep my commandments**.*

Here we read that GOD spoke all these words and reminded them to have no other gods or idols, to not worship or serve them....for THIS disobedience, he would visit the iniquity on the 3rd and 4th generation. However, GOD would show mercy to those that "LOVE HIM" and "KEEP HIS COMMANDMENTS". SO...UNLESS you are worshipping and serving other gods, you are NOT UNDER A CURSE. It's pretty clear here.

God never left the Israelites (a nation) without hope or mercy...HE is LOVE and MERCY...which always overshadows judgment. It seems that God dealt with the nation of Israel as a whole entire nation...(i.e.: Joshua 7:1, 11-15).

But we also read about his hope and forgiveness that was made available to them in the following verses if they choose to confess:

Leviticus 26:39-42-39 And they that are left of you shall pine away in their iniquity in your enemies' lands; and also in the iniquities of their fathers shall they pine away with them.40 If they shall confess their iniquity, and the iniquity of their fathers, with their trespass which they trespassed against me, and that also they have walked contrary unto me;41 And that I also have walked contrary unto them, and have brought them into the land of their enemies; if then their uncircumcised hearts be humbled, and they then accept of the punishment of their iniquity

:⁴² Then will I remember my covenant with Jacob, and also my covenant with Isaac, and also my covenant with Abraham will I remember; and I will remember the land.

Numbers 14:19-21 ¹⁹ Pardon, I beseech thee, the iniquity of this people according unto the greatness of thy mercy, and as thou hast forgiven this people, from Egypt even until now.²⁰ And the LORD said, I have pardoned according to thy word:²¹ But as truly as I live, all the earth shall be filled with the glory of the LORD.

There are some that teach that a generational curse is only handed down to non-Christian family members; once a person accepts Christ, he is free. They also teach that a child can be inhabited by the "family demon", which can remain dormant until awakened by sin. The cure is to repent of sin and remove the demon.

Let us dig further into the BIBLE:

*Jeremiah 31:29-34 ²⁹ In those days they shall say no more, The fathers have eaten a sour grape, and the children's teeth are set on edge.³⁰ **But every one shall die for his own iniquity:** every man that eateth the sour grape, his teeth shall be set on edge.³¹ Behold, the days come, saith the LORD, that **I will make a new covenant** with the house of Israel, and with the house of Judah:³² **Not according to the covenant that I made with their fathers** in the day that I took them by the hand to bring them out of the land of Egypt; which my covenant* *they brake, although I was an husband unto them, saith the LORD:³³ But **this shall be the covenant that I will make with the house of Israel; After those days**, saith the LORD, I will put my law in their inward parts, and write it in their hearts; and will be their God, and they shall be my people.³⁴ And they shall teach no more every man his neighbour, and every man his brother, saying, Know the LORD: for they shall all know me, from the least of them unto the greatest of them, saith the LORD: for **I will forgive their iniquity, and I will remember their sin no more.***

Here we see where the children are not punished for their father's evil and natural character…that each one will die for his own sin. We also have an introduction to the NEW Covenant where the "law" will be written in our hearts, and we will know God and HE will forgive our iniquity and remember our sin NO MORE!!

And the latest and greatest explanation to me is the follow scriptures:….

*Ezekiel 181-32 1 The word of the LORD came unto me again, saying,² What mean ye, that ye use this proverb concerning the land of Israel, saying, The fathers have eaten sour grapes, and the children's teeth are set on edge?³ As I live, saith the Lord GOD, ye shall not have occasion any more to use this proverb in Israel.⁴ **Behold, all souls are mine; as the soul of the father, so also the soul of the son is mine: the soul that sinneth, it shall die.⁵ But if a man be just, and do that which is lawful and right,⁶ And hath not** eaten upon the mountains,*

64

neither hath lifted up his eyes to the idols of the house of Israel, neither hath defiled his neighbour's wife, neither hath come near to a menstruous woman, [7] And hath not oppressed any, but hath restored to the debtor his pledge, hath spoiled none by violence, hath given his bread to the hungry, and hath covered the naked with a garment; [8] He that hath not given forth upon usury, neither hath taken any increase, that hath withdrawn his hand from iniquity, hath executed true judgment between man and man, [9] Hath walked in my statutes, and hath kept my judgments, to deal truly; he is just, **he shall surely live***, saith the Lord GOD. [10]* **If he beget a son that is a** *robber, a shedder of blood, and that doeth the like to any one of these things, [11] And that doeth not any of those duties, but even hath eaten upon the mountains, and defiled his neighbour's wife, [12] Hath oppressed the poor and needy, hath spoiled by violence, hath not restored the pledge, and hath lifted up his eyes to the idols, hath committed abomination, [13] Hath given forth upon usury, and hath taken increase: shall he then live? he shall not live*: **he hath done all these abominations; he shall surely die; his blood shall be upon him.** *[14] Now, lo, if he beget a son, that seeth all his father's sins which he hath done, and considereth, and doeth not such like, [15] That hath not eaten upon the mountains, neither hath lifted up his eyes to the idols of the house of Israel, hath not defiled his neighbour's wife, [16] Neither hath oppressed any, hath not withholden the pledge, neither hath spoiled by violence, but hath given his bread to the hungry, and hath covered* the naked with a garment,[17] That hath taken off his hand from the poor, that hath not received usury nor increase, hath executed my judgments, hath walked in my statutes; he shall not die for the iniquity of his father, he shall surely live.[18] As for his father, because he cruelly oppressed, spoiled his brother by violence, and did that which is not good among his people, lo, even he shall die in his iniquity.[19] Yet say ye, Why? **doth not the son bear the iniquity of the father? When the son hath done that which is lawful and right, and hath kept all my statutes, and hath done them, he shall surely live.[20] The soul that sinneth, it shall die. The son shall not bear the iniquity of the father, neither shall the father bear the iniquity of the son: the righteousness of the righteous shall be upon him, and the wickedness of the wicked shall be upon him.**[21] But if the wicked will turn from all his sins that he hath committed, and keep all my statutes, and do that which is lawful and right, he shall surely live, he shall not die.[22] All his transgressions that he hath committed, they shall not be mentioned unto him: in his righteousness that he hath done he shall live.[23] Have I any pleasure at all that the wicked should die? saith the Lord GOD: and not that he should return from his ways, and live?[24] But when the righteous turneth away from his righteousness, and committeth iniquity, and doeth according to all the abominations that the wicked man doeth, shall he live? All his righteousness that he hath done shall not be mentioned: in his trespass that he hath trespassed, and in his sin that he hath sinned, in them shall he die.[25] Yet ye say, The way of the LORD is not equal. Hear now, O house of Israel; Is not my way equal? are not your ways

66

*unequal?²⁶ When a righteous man turneth away from his righteousness, and committeth iniquity, and dieth in them; for his iniquity that he hath done shall he die.²⁷ Again, when the wicked man turneth away from his wickedness that he hath committed, and doeth that which is lawful and right, he shall save his soul alive.²⁸ Because **he considereth, and turneth away from all his transgressions that he hath committed, he shall surely live, he shall not die.**²⁹ Yet saith the house of Israel, The way of the LORD is not equal. O house of Israel, are not my ways equal? are not your ways unequal?³⁰ **Therefore I will judge you, O house of Israel, every one according to his ways,** saith the Lord GOD. Repent, and turn yourselves from all your transgressions; so iniquity shall not be your ruin.³¹ Cast away from you all your transgressions, whereby ye have transgressed; and make you a new heart and a new spirit: for why will ye die, O house of Israel?³² For I have no pleasure in the death of him that dieth, saith the Lord GOD: wherefore turn yourselves, and live ye.*

SOOOOOO...........we clearly see here that we are all responsible for our own spiritual walk...the SON does not inherit death because of what his father has done.

Can we please understand that we are NOW in a NEW covenant...where ALL things are made new...and where the BLOOD OF JESUS is enough to REDEEM us back to LIFE in CHRIST…back to SONSHIP with our heavenly Father!

More on living a LIFE IN CHRIST…FULL OF GRACE and MERCY.

God took away the old covenant and established the new.

Hebrews 10:9-10 ⁹ Then said he, Lo, I come to do thy will, O God. He taketh away the first, that he may **establish the second.**¹⁰ *By the which* **will we are sanctified through the offering of the body of Jesus Christ once for all.**

IT IS FINISHED….Let us labor to "REST" in the finished work of JESUS CHRIST!!

JESUS IS ENOUGH!!

CHAPTER SEVEN

CHRISTIAN CULTS

Are You In a Christian Cult?

□ □ □

I am seeing more and more of a certain "trend" among some Christian Groups. I have started to recognize some signs that could be defined as "cultish traits". I write this as a warning because a lot of us can get caught up in promoting or becoming "cultish" without ever realizing it. Most people who are caught up in cults or following a cult leader NEVER REALIZE IT!! There are some of these groups right here in my own community, and I want to just ask you to be more aware of what or whom you align yourself with. The Bible tells us to **"know those that labor among us"** ...

1 Thessalonians 5:12 And we beseech you, brethren, ***to know them which labour among you,*** *and are over you in the Lord, and admonish you;*

I will attempt to list simply a FEW of these traits and if you see any of these in the Group, Church, or Ministry that you are a part of or following, I would ask you to just be cautious of giving them too much influence in your life.

Characteristics of a Cult:

- There is **ONLY ONE** TEACHER, Preacher, Apostle or Prophet that is allowed to teach or speak on whatever platform is being used. It is a ONE MAN or ONE WOMAN show.
- The TEACHER, Preacher, Apostle or PROPHET is the **ONLY ONE** who has this super-spiritual or *super-natural* **KNOWLEDGE** or WISDOM and all the others can or will never ACHIEVE this status. God only speaks "REVELATIONS" to them.
- The members are to SUBMIT or be in SUBJECTION to their TEACHER, Preacher, Apostle or PROPHET and to OBEY and DO WHAT THEY SAY without question. This is ALL about ESTABLISHING CONTROL over you through MANIPULATION of your emotions, finances or spiritual beliefs.
- There is ONLY ONE CURICULUUM to be used, and all others are not allowed.
- You will NEVER be TAUGHT to EXCEL in the AREA of EDUCATION…their goal is to keep you at a lower level to keep the ARM of CONTROL over you.
- You are NOT ALLOWED to DISAGREE or even QUESTION there teachings, or ideas. IF or WHEN you DO QUESTION what they believe the LEADER of the GROUP will become ANGRY and DEFENSIVE.
- You are kept ISOLATED and never allowed to go outside this church, denomination, click or group. If you LEAVE you are immediately

EXCOMMUNICATED, and "CAST OUT",
blocked and treated as an unbeliever or heretic,
and NOT ALLOWED to have FELLOWSHIP
or COMMUNICATION with the GROUP or
Church. You are now labeled even an
"apostate" and "wicked person".

- When you LEAVE you will be SHAMED or
MADE FUN of by the WHOLE GROUP who
is still in the Church, or Group. You will even
be SHAMED in front of THE GROUP
LEADERS when EXCOMMUNICATED.

- When you are EXCOMMUNICATED...even
after years of being in the church or GROUP,
you will be sent out with NOTHING or little
to NOTHING....maybe not even a phone call
to family to come and pick you up after they
just put you and your few bags "on the curb".

- You are asked to FINANCIALLY SUPPORT
your TEACHER, Preacher, Apostle or
PROPHET...and to in no way QUESTION
WHERE or HOW your financial contributions
are being spent, even at the DEMISE of your
OWN Financial Health or prosperity.

- You may even be asked to RELENQUISH
ALL YOUR PERSONAL POSESSIONS or
FINANCES to the GROUP, Church or Leader
upon entry to the church or group.

- You may be asked to WORK for a BELOW
LIVING WAGE level just so you can "earn
your keep"...with the promise they will put a

little away in your savings. This again is to keep you under their arm of CONTROL.

- You may be asked to GIVE UP your GOVERNMENT INCOME to contribute to your living expenses…or even told to give it up permanently.
- You may be asked to DO THINGS that you KNOW GO AGAINST your NORMAL MORAL COMPASS.
- You will be asked to OBEY a MAN MADE DOCTRINE or IDEOLOGY that DOES NOT AGREE with the HOLY BIBLE.
- You will be asked to COMMIT SUICIDE to become a martyr for your spiritual beliefs or ideology.

I encourage you, IF you are seeing ANY of these SIGNS, or IF you are seeing MORE than one of these SIGNS, I beg you to consider creating some "DISTANCE" between you and the TEACHER, PROPHET, Apostle, Pastor, church or GROUP that is exhibiting these signs. It is for your own spiritual, emotional and financial HEALTH and WELL BEING that you GUARD yourself against those that are out to create their own "CULT FOLLOWING".

The words of Apostle Paul remind me here of what a TRUE "overseer's" heart looks like even before he is ready to depart from his brethren, the elders of the church, on the next road in his journey:……

Acts 20: 24 "But I do not consider my life of any account as dear to myself, so that I may finish my course *and the ministry which I received from the Lord Jesus, to testify solemnly of the gospel of the grace of God. 25 "And now, behold, I know that all of you, among whom I went about preaching the kingdom, will no longer see my face. 26 "Therefore, I testify to you this day that I am innocent of the blood of all men. 27 **"For I did not shrink from declaring to you the whole purpose of God.** 28 "Be on guard for yourselves and for all the flock, among which the Holy Spirit has made you **overseers**, to **shepherd the church of God** which He purchased with His own blood. 29 "I know that after my departure savage wolves will come in among you, not sparing the flock; 30 and from among your own selves men will arise, speaking perverse things, to draw away the disciples after them. 31 "Therefore be on the alert, remembering that night and day for a period of three years I did not cease to admonish each one with tears. 32 "And now I commend you to God and to the word of His grace, which is able to build you up and to give you the inheritance among all those who are sanctified. 33 "I have coveted no one's silver or gold or clothes. 34 "You yourselves know that these hands ministered to my own needs and to the men who were with me. 35 "In everything I showed you that by working hard in this manner you must help the weak and remember the words of the Lord Jesus, that He Himself said, 'It is more blessed to give than to receive.'"*

I pray that we **WATCH and PRAY** as there are many that are seeking to GAIN DISCIPLES to FOLLOW

THEM and NOT to FOLLOW JESUS! I pray that we WATCH over our minds that can be corrupted from the "SIMPLICITY that is IN CHRIST"! I pray that we WATCH OUT for those that are PREACHING ANOTHER GOSPEL or MANIFESTING ANOTHER SPIRIT!

*2 Corinthians 11:3 But I fear, lest by any means, as the serpent beguiled Eve through his subtilty, so your minds should be corrupted from the simplicity that is in Christ. 4 For if he that cometh preacheth another Jesus, whom we have not preached, or if ye receive **another spirit**, which ye have not received, or **another gospel**, which ye have not accepted, ye might well bear with him.*

Let us really take the time we need to get to KNOW those that LABOR among us before we completely ALIGN OURSELVES with someone or something that can come disguised as an "Angel of Light"…yet will lead us down a PATH or HURT and SPIRITUAL DEATH.

*2 Corinthians 11:13 For such are false apostles, deceitful workers, **transforming themselves into the apostles of Christ**. 14 And no marvel; for **Satan himself is transformed into an angel of light**. 15 Therefore it is no great thing if his ministers also be transformed as the ministers of righteousness; whose end shall be according to their works.*

I pray that we all receive the Spirit of Truth …which will LEAD and GUIDE us INTO ALL TRUTH….JESUS!!!

74

*John 16:13 Howbeit when he, the **Spirit of truth**, is come, **he will guide you into all truth**: for **he shall not speak of himself**; but whatsoever he shall hear, that shall he speak: and he will shew you things to come. 14 **He shall glorify me**: for he shall receive of mine, and **shall shew it unto you.***

John 14:⁶ Jesus saith unto him, I am the way, the truth, and the life: no man cometh unto the Father, but by me.

JESUS is the ONLY ONE I want to FOLLOW and JESUS is the ONLY ONE I should be POINTING PEOPLE TO!! JESUS...HE is the WAY, the **TRUTH** and the LIFE!!

CHAPTER EIGHT

SPIRITUAL WARFARE

*Binding and Loosing...Should You Do
It?*

☐ ☐ ☐

In this Chapter we will take a look at another highly controversial topic that has also encountered much debate regarding "binding" and "loosing".

We will examine Matthew 18:15-35. There is so much in these passages. Jesus is the one speaking here to his disciples about what to do if a brother trespasses against them. These verses are about how the church should handle offense through a church discipline process, and how to move into forgiveness as your Father in heaven forgives you.

For reference I want to also point out some official rabbinic terms and culture of the time and will take an excerpt from google's Wikipedia to help educate us on that here...

Binding and loosing is originally a Jewish Mishnaic phrase also mentioned in the New Testament, as well as in the Targum. In usage, *to bind* and *to loose* simply means *to forbid by an indisputable authority* and *to permit by an indisputable authority*. One example of this is Isaiah 58:5-6 which relates proper fasting to loosing the chains of injustice.

The "poseks" had, by virtue of their ordination, the power of deciding disputes relating to Jewish law. Hence, the difference between the two main schools of thought in early classical Judaism were summed up by the phrase *the school of Shammai binds; the school of Hillel looses.*

Theoretically, however, the authority of the poseks proceeded from the Sanhedrin, and there is therefore a Talmudic statement that there were **three** decisions made by the *lower house of judgment* (the Sanhedrin) to which the *upper house of judgment* (the heavenly one) gave its *supreme sanction.* The claim that *whatsoever [a disciple] bind[s] or loose[s] on earth shall be bound or loosed in heaven,* which the Gospel of Matthew attributes to Jesus, is probably therefore just an adoption of a phrase popular at the time.

This is also the meaning of the phrase when it is applied in the text to Simon Peter and the other apostles in particular when they are invested with the power to bind and loose by Christ.

First evidence of binding and loosening:

Acts Chapter 15 expresses the first documented instance of loosening and binding; what has been later termed the Council at Jerusalem. Here the early controversy of circumcision was resolved, and loosened from being a qualification for salvation and acceptance into the community of believers. In the depiction below, we see an appeal to follow what has been revealed by the Holy Spirit, and not what opinions of men would suppose.

*Acts 15:1 Certain men came down from Judea and were teaching the brethren: "Unless you are circumcised, according to the custom taught by Moses, you cannot be saved." 2 This brought Paul and Barnabas into sharp dispute and debate with them. So **Paul and Barnabas were appointed**, along **with some other believers**, to go up to Jerusalem **to see the apostles and elders about this question**. 3 The church sent them on their way, and as they traveled through Phoenicia and Samaria, they told how the Gentiles had been converted. This news made all the believers very glad. 4 When they came to Jerusalem, they were welcomed by the church and the apostles and elders, to whom they reported everything God had done through them. 5 Then some of the believers who belonged to the party of the Pharisees stood up and said, "The Gentiles must be circumcised and required to keep the law of Moses." 6 The **apostles and elders met to consider** this question. 7 After much discussion, **Peter** got up and addressed them: "Brothers, you know that some time ago God made a choice among you that the Gentiles might hear from my lips the message of the gospel and believe [first Gentile conversion, Acts 10]. 8 God, who* *knows the heart, showed that he accepted them by giving the Holy Spirit to them, just as he did to us. 9 He did not discriminate between us and them, for he purified their hearts by faith. 10 Now then, why do you try to test God by putting on the necks of Gentiles a yoke that neither we nor our ancestors have been able to bear? 11 No! We believe it is through the grace of our Lord Jesus that we are saved, just as they are."12 The whole assembly became silent as **they listened to Barnabas and Paul** telling about the signs and wonders God had done among the Gentiles through them. 13 When they finished, **James** spoke up. "Brothers," he said, "listen to me. 14 Simon has described to us how God first intervened to choose a people for his name from the Gentiles. 15 The words of the prophets are in agreement with this, as it is written:16 "'After this I will return and rebuild David's fallen tent. Its ruins I will rebuild, and I will restore it, 17 that the rest of mankind may seek the Lord, even all the Gentiles who bear my name, says the Lord, who does these things'— 18 things known from long ago.19 "**It is my judgment** [James speaking], therefore, that we should not make it difficult for the Gentiles who are turning to God. 20 Instead we should write to them, telling them to abstain from food polluted by idols, from sexual immorality, from the meat of strangled animals and from blood. 21 For the law of Moses has been preached in every city from the earliest times and is read in the synagogues on every Sabbath."22 Then the **apostles and elders, with the whole church,***

79

decided to choose some of their own men and send them to Antioch with Paul and Barnabas. They chose Judas (called Barsabbas) and Silas, men who were leaders among the believers. 23 With them they sent the following letter:**The apostles and elders**, your brothers,To the Gentile believers in Antioch, Syria and Cilicia:Greetings. 24 We have heard that some went out from us without **our** authorization and disturbed you, troubling your minds by what they said. 25 So **we all agreed** to choose some men and send them to you with our dear friends Barnabas and Paul— 26 men who have risked their lives for the name of our Lord Jesus Christ. 27 Therefore we are sending Judas and Silas to **confirm by word of mouth what we are writing**. 28 **It seemed good to the Holy Spirit and to us not to burden you with anything beyond the following requirements**: 29 You are to abstain from food sacrificed to idols, from blood, from the meat of strangled animals and from sexual immorality. You will do well to avoid these things. Farewell.30 So the men were sent off and went down to Antioch, where they gathered the church together and delivered the letter. 31 The people read it and were glad for its encouraging message. 32 Judas and Silas, who themselves were prophets, said much to encourage and strengthen the believers. 33 After spending some time there, they were sent off by the believers with the blessing of peace to return to those who had sent them. 35 But Paul and Barnabas remained in Antioch, where they and many others taught and preached the word of the Lord.

Controversy still exists today whether the authority to loosen or bind is still in effect, if it passed at some point during the church's early development, or to what extent Gospel and doctrine have been loosened or bound by either the Catholic, Eastern Orthodox, Coptic Orthodox, Protestant and other traditions.

So with ALL of this information and Jewish laws and traditions and sects, I encourage you to study and examine this deeper if you have any questions, and there is a lot to learn.

Moving on let us examine what Matthew 18 is really referring to in my best opinion. Remember this is Jesus speaking…

Matthew 18: [15] *Moreover if thy brother shall **trespass against thee**, go and tell him his fault between thee and him **alone**: if he shall hear thee, thou hast gained thy brother.*

Here we see that if there is a sin or trespass from a brother (believer) against us (the body of Christ), if someone hurt us or is in sin, we are to go directly to him ALONE, and tell him what the issue is. If he hears us, we have gained a brother. Some may say this would be step one in church discipline in bringing the brother to repentance and reconciliation between us (the body) and the brother who was in sin.

*Matthew 18: [16] But if he will not hear thee, then take with thee one or two more, that in the **mouth of two or three witnesses** every word may be established.*

Here we see that if step one doesn't work to bring repentance, forgiveness and reconciliation with our brother, we should take one or two more with us so that our words will be established or heard from this brother who has sinned against us. We see this also spoken by Paul in 2 Corinthians 13:1 when he was bringing rebuke and correction to those that had sinned. We also read in... *Deuteronomy 19: [15] **One witness shall not rise up against a man for any iniquity**, or for any sin, in any sin that he sinneth: at the **mouth of two witnesses, or at the mouth of three witnesses, shall the matter be established**.*

So that the sin or iniquity is brought to the brother who trespassed so it will be established, this could be considered step two in church discipline.

*Matthew 18: [17] And if he shall **neglect to hear them**, tell it unto the church: but if he neglect to hear the church, let him be unto thee as an heathen man and a publican.*

Step three in church discipline is that if the brother in trespass or sin neglects to hear "them" that we are to tell it unto the church so that the whole assembly may help the brother come to repentance. If he continues to not hear the church (assembly) then he should be viewed as a heathen or a publican (tax collector)...an unbeliever, even excommunicated from the church.

We also read in 1 Timothy 5:19-20 this type of church discipline process is encouraged.

Matthew 18: [18]*Verily I say unto you, Whatsoever ye shall bind on earth shall be bound in heaven: and whatsoever ye shall loose on earth shall be loosed in heaven.*

Here we as the church do not have the ability to determine what is right or wrong, good or evil…only the Word of God has that authority. We are to declare the judgment of Heaven based on God's Word and all Heaven will be in accord with His Word. If a brother confesses and repents of his trespass, then we can see where he is loosed from his sin or trespass. If he does not repent, his forgiveness is bound to his sin. So whatever we bind on Earth shall be bound in Heaven and whatever we loose on Earth will be loosed in Heaven.

Matthew 18: [19]*Again I say unto you, That if two of you shall agree on earth as touching any thing that they shall ask, it shall be done for them of my Father which is in heaven.* [20]*For where two or three are gathered together in my name, there am I in the midst of them.*

We see here that where we are in agreement according to his word, He is willing to confirm what the Word of God allows and says.

Matthew 18: ²¹ *Then came Peter to him, and said,* **Lord, how oft shall my brother sin against me, and I forgive him**? *till seven times?*²² *Jesus saith unto him, I say not unto thee, Until seven times: but, Until seventy times seven.*²³ *Therefore is the kingdom of heaven likened unto a certain king, which would take account of his servants.*²⁴ *And when he had begun to reckon, one was brought unto him, which owed him ten thousand talents.*²⁵ *But forasmuch as he had not to pay, his lord commanded him to be sold, and his wife, and children, and all that he had, and payment to be made.*²⁶ *The servant therefore fell down, and worshipped him, saying, Lord, have patience with me, and I will pay thee all.*²⁷ *Then the lord of that servant was moved with compassion, and loosed him, and forgave him the debt.*²⁸ *But the same* **servant** *went out, and found one of his fellowservants, which owed him an hundred pence: and he laid hands on him, and took him by the throat, saying, Pay me that thou owest.*²⁹ *And his fellowservant fell down at his feet, and besought him, saying, Have* **patience with me,** *and I will pay thee all.*³⁰ *And* **he would not**: *but went and* **cast him into prison**, *till he should pay the debt.*³¹ *So when his fellowservants saw what was done, they were very sorry, and came and told unto their lord all that was done.*³² *Then his* **lord**, *after that he had* **called** *him, said unto him, O thou* **wicked servant**, *I forgave thee all that debt, because thou desiredst me:*³³ **Shouldest not thou also have had compassion on thy fellowservant,** *even as I had pity on thee?*³⁴ *And his lord was wroth, and delivered him to the tormentors, till he should pay all that was due unto him.*³⁵ *So likewise shall my heavenly Father*

84

do also unto you, if ye from your hearts forgive not every one his brother their trespasses.

Here Jesus continues to speak to Peter who asked in continuance of the lesson on resolving a trespass or offence, how many times he should forgive…Jesus tells Peter "seventy time seven"…pretty much to mean "unlimited" forgiveness as he demonstrated by the following parable of the Lord and wicked servant that did not forgive his fellow servants. Jesus in verse 33 admonished them to have "compassion on thy fellow servant" as the Lord had pity on him. Jesus also said that if you from your hearts do not forgive everyone their trespasses, then likewise the heavenly Father will also do unto you.

So to summarize this whole passage we see it is about Jesus first taking a Judaic tradition of church discipline and talks about using this process to try and bring a lost brother to reconciliation, and summarizes it with forgiveness. This chapter is NOT a formula for spiritual warfare to use to directly "bind or loose" the devil.

Please stop bringing a "railing accusation" directly to the devil (a fallen angel) while you are still living in your "mortal" body. You are asking for a full on attack, physically, spiritually and emotionally. I admonish you to go to Jesus, ask Him, the Lord to rebuke satan. There is only "ONE" mediator between God and Man that is JESUS!

Use wisdom...stop teaching things from your own "vain imaginations" ...it is dangerous to do this, please.

CHAPTER NINE

WHO IS THE THIEF?

Do You Know Who REALLY Came to
Kill, Steal and Destroy?

□   □   □

Who is the THIEF? We have a habit of just "echoing" what we hear other Christians say without actually reading, studying or looking it up for ourselves to see if this is what we are just repeating is true? We are like little parrots...just "talking, talking, and talking" without ever speaking truth. I, myself, have been guilty of doing this.

So today we are going to examine John 10. We often misquote verse 10 as saying "the thief" that comes to steal, kill and destroy is "the devil". This is not truly what this is referring to. Let us back up and look at the verses prior to this all the way back to verse 1.

*John 10:10 Verily, verily, I say unto you, **He that enphtereth not by the door** into the sheepfold, but climbeth up some other way, the same **is a thief** and a robber.² But he that entereth in by the door is the shepherd of the sheep.³ To him the porter openeth; and the sheep hear his voice: and he calleth his own sheep by name, and leadeth* *them out.⁴ And when he putteth forth his own sheep, he goeth before them, and the sheep follow him: for they know his voice.⁵ And a stranger will they not follow, but will flee from him: for they know not the voice of strangers.⁶ This parable spake Jesus unto them: but they understood not what things they were which he spake unto them.⁷ Then said **Jesus unto them** again, Verily, verily, I say unto you, **I am the door** of the sheep.⁸ **All that ever came before me are thieves** and robbers: but the sheep did not hear them.⁹ I am the door: by me if any man enter in, he shall be saved, and shall go in and out, and find pasture.¹⁰ The **thief** cometh not, but for to steal, and to kill, and to destroy: I am come that they might have life, and that they might have it more abundantly.¹¹ I am the good shepherd: the good shepherd giveth his life for the sheep.¹² But **he that is an hireling**, and **not the shepherd**, whose own the sheep are not, seeth the wolf coming, and **leaveth the sheep, and fleeth**: and the wolf catcheth them, and scattereth the sheep.¹³ The **hireling fleeth,** because he is an hireling, and **careth not for the sheep**.¹⁴ I am the good shepherd, and know my sheep, and am known of mine.¹⁵ As the Father knoweth me, even so know I the Father: and I lay down my life for the sheep.¹⁶ And other sheep I have, which are not of this fold: them also I must bring, and they shall hear my voice; and there shall be one fold, and one shepherd.*

In verse 10 the "thief" tries to enter into the kingdom by another way other than Jesus, and convinces others by his voice, words or teachings to do the same, and robs people of eternal life and salvation.

We see here...the "thief" is "the hireling" or false teacher that teaches for money, that is sent to lead the flock away from the true shepherd, the door...Jesus, the TRUTH. The thief cares nothing for the sheep and is just someone that can be "hired" for his own gain. So my advice again is to really discern who you align yourself with as your teacher.

The enemy, the devil, of course is the one behind the "hireling" and "false teachers" using their own vanity and selfish greed against the body of Christ. We are warned over and over in the New Testaments about false teachers, prophets, apostles and even a false "spirit". Please stay in the Word of God ONLY; it is your "truth plumb line".

CHAPTER TEN

COVERING

*WHO is your SPIRITUAL head,
authority or covering?*

□ □ □

This has been such a sticky and controversial issue, as man is always looking to acquire power and rule over man. Some Christians believe that they need a "protective covering", that protects them from doctrinal error, moral failure and even an attack from satan.

It is true we need mature Biblical leaders to oversee sound doctrine, but a "man" who is fallible is not our spiritual "headship" or covering.

The word "covering" only appears once in the entire New Testament in 1 Corinthians 11:15 and we mentioned this in a previous chapter. Covering here refers to a veil or head covering, and it is never used to denote a "spiritual covering". It is never used to give a Leader/Pastor authority OVER another man or woman or the "layman". The pastor is then held accountable by his "denominational headquarter" or "movement/ organization" that he is licensed with. So it is a "hierarchical" authority, top-down leadership model.

This "positional" model is a worldly system, and cannot be supported biblically in the New Testament. The positional mindset uses terms like "pastor", "prophet", "bishop", "apostle", which are titles representing ecclesiastical offices. An office is a sociological slot/office that a group defines apart from the person that fills it. However in the New Testament we can see the leadership represents not "an office" but a "function" in activities such as "pastoring", "prophesying", "overseeing"…not just a title.

The Bible does not give mankind dominion or authority over man, again look at Genesis. When someone asks, "Who is your covering", they are in essence asking "who controls you"? As we begin to study we will read that we are only accountable to GOD…and Jesus Christ is the HEAD of HIS body the church, HE is our preeminence, our High Priest, our King.

*Romans 14:12 So then every one of us shall give **account of himself to God**.*

*Colossians 1:18 And he is the **head of the body,** the church: who is the beginning, the **firstborn** from the dead; that in all things he might have the **preeminence**.*

*Hebrews 4:14 Seeing then that we have a great **high priest,** that is passed into the heavens, **Jesus** the Son of God, let us hold fast our profession.*

91

*John 18:37 Pilate therefore said unto him, Art thou a king then? **Jesus answered**, Thou sayest that **I am a king. To this end was I born**, and for this cause came I into the world, that I should bear witness unto the truth. Every one that is of the **truth heareth my voice**.*

I say first and foremost we consider the words of Jesus and see what he has to say about it in Matthew 20:25-28. But let's go back to the beginning to start.

When we first study the book of Genesis 1:26 we read where God made mankind in his image and he gave "them" dominion over...MAN? NO!!! He gave them dominion over the fish of the sea, and over the fowl of the air, and over the cattle, and over all the earth, and over every creeping thing that creepeth upon the earth. The Bible then goes on to tell us in verse 27 that God created mankind in his **own** image, in the image of God created he him; **male and female** created he **them**. So the "**them**" God gave dominion to was BOTH male and female. We also can read the rest in verse 28 where God blessed **them**, and God said unto **them**, Be fruitful, and multiply, and replenish the earth, and subdue it: and have **dominion OVER** the fish of the sea, and over the fowl of the air, and over every **living thing** that moveth upon the earth. We sum up Chapter 1 in verse 31 by seeing that God saw everything that he had made, and behold, it was **very good**. And the evening and the morning were the **sixth** day.

Then all hell broke loose, and Adam and Eve sinned against God by their disobedience...we call this the Fall.

After the Fall in Chapter 3 we see God **curse** the serpent in verse 14 and **curse** the ground in verse 17...and God pronounced to Adam and the woman a severe consequence along before He expelled them from the Garden of Eden. In verse 17-19 you can read the consequence for the man was a ground of thorns and thistles and hard work and for the woman we read in verse 16 she would in sorrow bring forth children and her desire would be to her husband, and he (her husband) shall **rule over thee** (her).

So we see here that the consequence of the sin of disobedience was that man would **RULE OVER** the woman. Could it be, that because of her sin, God gave her a necessary "headship"? It was NOT God's original plan for this...because he originally gave **them dominion over only the animals** and over every **living thing** that moved upon the earth...and **over all the earth itself**. We MUST read this as it was actually written in Genesis 1:26.

When we take a look at what JESUS SAID about "exercising dominion over" or "exercising authority upon someone" we will read a different mindset for the Kingdom Jesus came to bring.

In Matthew 20:20-28, we read a story about James and John's mother (of Zebedee's children) that came worshipping Jesus but we read in verse 20, that she desired something of him (Jesus). She wanted her two sons to have "seats of authority" in Jesus' kingdom…to sit on his right and left hand. Jesus answered and reminded her in verse 23 that this place of position was not His to give but would be given to them for who it was prepared of by His Father. The other ten disciples hear this interaction and they were moved with indignation against the two brethren. Jesus proceeds to go on and say a very monumental statement in verses 25-28. In *verse 25 it reads, "But Jesus called them unto him, and said, Ye know that the princes of the Gentiles exercise **dominion OVER them,** and they that are great exercise AUTHORITY UPON them, and then in verse 26 "But it shall NOT BE SO AMONG YOU: but whosoever will be great among you, let him be your minister; verse 27 And whosoever will be chief among you, let him be your servant: verse 28 Even as the Son of man came NOT to be ministered unto, but to minister, and to give his life a ransom for many.*

Let's look at just a few other scriptures, and I pray that you will discern what Jesus' heart was in the scriptures you just read in Matthew 20.

As we deal with the passage in Hebrews 13:7, 17, 24, the word "**rule**" is translated from the Greek word "*hegeomai*" and it means "**to guide or go before**", so it can be thought to say "those that guide you" rather than "those that rule over you".

In 1 Thessalonians 5:12, the word "**over**" is translated from the Greek word "*proistemi*" and the idea of this word means "standing in front of, superintending,

guarding, and **providing care**". So if we read it in that meaning it reads as, "And we beseech you brethren, to know them which labor (work hard) among you, and are over **(care for)** you in the Lord, and admonish you; and verse 13 continues to state to esteem them very highly in love for their work's sake.

We also see Paul's instruction to bishop's (overseer's) in 1 Timothy 3:4-5 admonishes them to "ruleth" (guide) well his own house, having his children in subjection (under obedience) with all gravity.

The passages come from a place of watching or guarding over, superintending or overseeing, facilitating and guiding **rather than ruling over**. If we can imagine a "true shepherd" who guards his flock, caring for it from a place of "servant hood" with all humility who looks out for their well being and gently leads them versus driving them from behind or over them from above.

Let us also look at being "ordained" by man for an office of Apostle. In Titus 1:5 the word "ordain" is translated in the Greek as "*kathistemi*'…and means "**to set**". In Acts 14:23 the word "ordained" is "*kirotoneo*" means "**to stretch forth the hand**". It does not confirm Biblical authority by a man. It means to acknowledge those that have already been endorsed by the Holy Spirit. Ordination is a public outward confirmation by the church body of those that the Holy Spirit has already selected.

*Acts 20:28 Take heed therefore unto yourselves, and to all the flock, over the which the **Holy Ghost hath made you overseers**, to feed the church of God, which he hath purchased with his own blood.*

When we attach spiritual recognition of elders to special "ordination" ceremonies, minister licenses, college/seminary degrees, we are instituting man's worldly recognition versus true biblical teaching.

We are to recognize the elders in a sense of their "function" versus placing into an official "office".

In Ephesians 4:7-8 we clearly see that Christ is the one who gives "gifts" (apostles, prophets, evangelists, pastors and teachers) unto men…that it is NOT man that appoints them to the Body.

I hope this brings a little clarity to the forefront of this "office" or "positional" authority or ruling over.

We can read all the Gospels in how Jesus came to bring the only **real REFORMATION**. He came to bring a "new" covenant…JESUS was our HIGH PRIEST, Hebrews 9:11, by a greater and more perfect tabernacle, not made with hands, that is to say, NOT of this building. JESUS is the HEAD of HIS body, THE CHURCH, Colossians 1:18, and that in ALL things He (JESUS) might have the PREEMINENCE!

CHAPTER ELEVEN

TONGUES

Just for Corporate Worship...or
MORE?

□   □   □

The subject of "speaking in other tongues" is so widely misrepresented or only glossed over without utilizing ALL the Bible verses regarding this subject. I would like to again, bring a little more clarity to this issue.

Unfortunately, a lot of amazing Biblical scholars and theologians with such an amazing mind only filter the scriptures through their "doctrinal" belief system, and tend to leave out all the other scriptures where tongues are discussed out of their teachings.

Let us look at some scriptures:

Isaiah 28:11 For with stammering lips and another tongue will he speak to this people.

Here we see it mentioned in the Old Testament that God will speak to His people this way...with "another tongue" and "stammering lips". So should we be afraid of it, if it is how God chooses to speak to us?

Acts 2:4 And they were all filled with the Holy Ghost, and began to speak with other tongues, as the Spirit gave them utterance.

Here we see what happened on the day of Pentecost in the book of Acts. When we read what Jesus said to them in Acts 1:4-5 he told them to go "wait for the promise of the Father", and said they would be "baptized with the Holy Ghost not many days hence". We see where there were 120 waiting in an upper room for this promise and on the day of Pentecost it says in Acts 2:2-3 *And suddenly there came a sound from heaven as of a rushing might wind, and it filled all the house where they were sitting. 3 And there appeared unto them cloven tongues like as of fire, and it sat upon each of them.* In verse 4 they were filled with the Holy Ghost, and began to speak with other tongues as the **Spirit gave utterance**…it could not be given or taught by man. We see in verse 6 this tongues was different languages of the nations that were represented there so all could hear and understand what they were saying…in verse 11 it says they were speaking the "wonderful works of God". So the "understanding" of the languages was given to edify the whole group or body of people that were there. Of course immediately we see the doubters and mockers in verse 12-13 who came in making fun of and accusing them of being drunk. However Peter stood up **with** the other eleven Apostles and stated **"these are NOT drunken"**…to shut up the mockers who would degrade this event into something so carnal as "drunkenness". Why would God use a "drunken" manifestation or people to speak his wonderful works when the Bible tells us that "drunkards" won't inherit the Kingdom of God (1 Corinthians 6:9-10)? So Peter shut that down real quick, and reminded them in verse 16 that "this is that which was spoken by the prophet Joel;" (Joel 2:28). So he stated a prophecy of old was being fulfilled during this event. This prophecy in this event HAD been fulfilled.

The Book of Acts is filled with the Apostles preaching Christ and the outpouring of the Holy Ghost was happening. Here is another example of this in Acts 19...

*Acts 19:6 And when **Paul had laid his hands upon them**, the Holy Ghost came on them; and they **spake with tongues**, and prophesied.*

Jesus upon giving the Great Commission to the eleven Apostles stated this sign of being able to "speak with new tongues" would follow them that believe here in Mark 16. So if Jesus said it would happen to believers...why would we say it is not for us today?

*Mark 16:17 And these **signs** shall follow **them that believe**; In my name shall they cast out devils; they shall **speak with new tongues**;*

The most misquoted chapter in the Bible regarding the use of tongues in a corporate church setting is stated here in 1 Corinthians 14. I will highlight a few verses that are "left out" a lot of this teaching.

*1 Corinthians 14:2 For he that speaketh in an unknown tongue **speaketh not unto men, but unto God**: for **no man understandeth him**; howbeit in the spirit he speaketh mysteries.*

*Romans 8:26 Likewise the Spirit also helpeth our infirmities: for we know not what we should pray for as we ought: but the **Spirit itself maketh intercession** for us with **groanings which cannot be uttered**.*

This talks about another use for speaking or praying in tongues…that when we utilize this gift of tongues we allow the Holy Spirit to pray through us "mysteries" unto God. Also interesting to note, no man will understand him. This is a "heavenly" prayer language. There is also a time when we are grieved, burdened or have infirmities and we may not know what or even how we should pray as we ought, so the Holy Spirit will fall *upon us* and makes intercession for us with groanings. This can be known as a "travailing" prayer in the Spirit. This has happened to me when I have felt such a "burden" for something that the Holy Spirit dropped on me to use me in this gifting. It is literally a gut-wrenching groaning prayer in tongues. This is a prayer for intercession.

*1 Corinthians 14: [4] He that **speaketh in an unknown tongue edifieth himself**; but he that prophesieth edifieth the church. [5] I **would that ye all spake with tongues** but rather that ye prophesied: for greater is he that*

100

prophesieth than he that speaketh with tongues, except he interpret, that the **church may receive edifying**.

Here Paul is again trying to bring order to this Corinthian church and advise them that the goal for a corporate gathering or worship should be done with order and to help edify, exhort or comfort even the new or unbelievers that are in this service. We can also note that he does say there is a prayer in tongues that "edifies self"...this is known as your own personal prayer language that the Holy Spirit will use just to build you up personally.

In a **corporate** gathering he recommends that they prophesy so those that those that are there can understand what is being said. He does also state, **"I would that ye ALL SPAKE with TONGUES"**, notice he DOES NOT SAY, "I would that ye all NEVER SPEAK with tongues"! He does also clarify that in a corporate church gathering the gift of tongues can be used as long as it comes with an interpretation so the WHOLE BODY can understand what God is saying, otherwise it does not benefit or profit the brethren...thus his statement in verse 6. He continues to drive home his point that in a church service we need to not cause confusion or fear as a new believer will look at us as a barbarian (verse 11), but again we need to "excel to the edifying of the church" (verse 12). He also continues to say it is OK to pray in an unknown tongue (verse 14) and pray or sing in the spirit but also with understanding or interpretation. Otherwise again how will the new or "unlearned" person that occupied the room be able to give thanks and he does not understand what is being said (verse 16). As we continue to read here…Paul goes on to say:

1 Corinthians 14:18-22 **[18]** *I thank my God, I speak with tongues more than ye all.* **[19]** *Yet* **in the church** *I had rather* **speak** *five words* **with my understanding,** *that by my voice I might teach others also, than ten thousand words in an unknown tongue.* **[20]** *Brethren, be not children in understanding: howbeit in malice be ye children, but in understanding be men.*

Notice the Apostle Paul says that even he **"thanks God, he speaks with tongues more than them all".** Notice Paul never said, "I NEVER speak in tongues and I forbid it". So if Paul says he has this gift, how can it not be from God?

1 Corinthians 14:21-22 **[21]** *In the law it is written, With men of other tongues and other lips will I speak unto this people; and yet for all that will they not hear me, saith the Lord.* **[22]** *Wherefore* **tongues are for a sign,** *not to them that believe,* **but to them that believe not:** *but prophesying serveth not for them that believe not, but for them which believe.*

Paul then reminds them of the law as it is written in the Bible verse in Isaiah 28:11. He also reminds them that tongues were not a gift that was used as a sign for those that believe but for the unbelievers, again restating

102

what happened in Acts 2:4. He continues on to say in this corporate gathering that the gift of prophesying serves those that believe.

Paul continues to give the regulations for the ministry of spiritual gifts in the local church.

1 Corinthians 14:(23-40) **²³** *If therefore* **the whole church be come together into one place**, *and all speak with tongues, and* **there come in those that are unlearned, or unbelievers**, *will they not say that ye are mad?*

Again, his intent for this chapter is stated here in verse 23, that if the **whole church be come together into one place** not to utilize this gift of tongues without giving an interpretation as the **unlearned and unbelievers** will think you all are mad. They then will not receive an understanding of what God is speaking to His corporate body.

*1 Corinthians 14:*²⁴ *But if all prophesy, and there come in one that believeth not, or one unlearned, he is convinced of all, he is judged of all:*²⁵ *And thus are the secrets of his heart made manifest; and so falling down on his face he will worship God, and report that God is in you of a truth.*²⁶ **How is it then, brethren? when ye come together**, *every one of you hath a psalm, hath a doctrine, hath a tongue, hath a revelation, hath an interpretation.* **Let all things be done unto edifying**.

103

Paul here is giving instructions as to how to bring order that will edify those that are unlearned or do not believe. He states **"let all things be done unto edifying"**.

*1 Corinthians 14:(27 If any man speak in an unknown tongue, let it be by two, or at the most by three, and that by course; and let one interpret.28 But **if** there be no interpreter, let him keep silence in the church; and let him speak to himself, and to God.*

The "IF" here specifies that tongues without interpretation is the only reason for "silencing" the gift of tongues…in this corporate setting. This "corporate" tongue is given as a sign to unbelievers.

29 Let the prophets speak two or three, and let the other judge.30 If any thing be revealed to another that sitteth by, let the first hold his peace.31 For ye may all prophesy one by one, that all may learn, and all may be comforted.32 And the spirits of the prophets are subject to the prophets.33 **For God is not the author of confusion, but of peace, as in all churches of the saints.** *34 Let your women keep silence in the churches: for it is not permitted unto them to speak; but they are commanded to be under obedience as also saith the law.35 And if they will learn any thing, let them ask their husbands at home: for it is a shame for women to speak in the church.36 What? came the word of God out from you? or came it unto you only?37 If any man think himself to be a prophet, or spiritual, let him acknowledge that the things that I write unto you are the commandments of the Lord.38 But if any man be ignorant, let him be ignorant.39 Wherefore,* *brethren, covet to prophesy, and forbid not to speak with tongues.* [40] **Let all things be done decently and in order.**

So we can see more instructions in verses 27-40 to the church at Corinth that had new believers coming in to their worship services, and they were all bringing in their zeal of the Lord, as mentioned in verse 12 causing confusion and chaos as they were all speaking in tongues, prophesying and the women were speaking out and probably asking questions…when there should have been order in these services. We also see where Paul said in verse 39 "Wherefore, brethren, covet to prophesy, and **forbid NOT to SPEAK WITH TONGUES**." So Paul tells us here that in a church corporate setting we are to **not forbid** allowing this gift to flow…but that we should utilize it with order.

Paul summarized 1 Corinthians 14 in the last verse 40 by stating his motive and purpose as to all that is written in this whole Chapter …verse 40 says, "Let **ALL THINGS be done DECENTLY and IN ORDER**". This is the reason he was addressing this disruptive behavior and issue in the Corinthian church.

I pray this helps bring just some clarity to this issue, and again we will note that if it was demonic, I think Paul may have walked in and rebuked them all and asked them the question, "Who has bewitched you"?

CHAPTER TWELVE

DRINKING

Is It Permitted for Christians?...

☐ ☐ ☐

This is a very touchy subject. I do believe there are a lot of different viewpoints and studies on it. However, I do want to at least address what the Bible actually says about it.

Most conservative Christians will take the stance that they are to NEVER drink or touch alcohol. I completely admire and respect that. The issue comes in on whether it is a sin or will it keep us out of the Kingdom of God?

Galatians 5:19-21 ¹⁹ *Now the works of the flesh are manifest, which are these; Adultery, fornication, uncleanness, lasciviousness,* ²⁰ *Idolatry, witchcraft, hatred, variance, emulations, wrath, strife, seditions, heresies,* ²¹ *Envyings, murders,* **drunkenness,** *revellings, and such like: of the which I tell you before, as I have also told you in time past, that* **they which do such things shall not inherit the kingdom of God.**

In Galatians it makes it clear that "drunkards" or those who participate in "drunkenness" won't inherit the

Kingdom of God. It's pretty clear here. How do you define "drunkenness"? The Greek word here is *"methe"* which means "intoxication". So for each individual, the amount that one drinks to get to a place of intoxication or being tipsy can be different based on your size and weight or tolerance level. This is something only you will know.

Let us also examine the following verses in whole:

1 Corinthians 6:9-12 *[9] Know ye not that **the unrighteous shall not inherit the kingdom of God?** Be not deceived: neither fornicators, nor idolaters, nor adulterers, nor effeminate, nor abusers of themselves with mankind, [10] Nor thieves, nor covetous, **nor drunkards**, nor revilers, nor extortioners, **shall inherit the kingdom of God.** [11] And such were some of you: **but ye are washed, but ye are sanctified, but ye are justified in the name of the Lord Jesus, and by the Spirit of our God.** [12] All things are lawful unto me, but all things are not expedient: all things are lawful for me, but I will not be brought under the power of any.*

Here we read where Paul lists the unrighteous acts of the people and again states they will not inherit the Kingdom of God. But he goes on to remind us...BUT ye are washed, sanctified and **justified** in the name of the Lord Jesus and by the Spirit of our God. He also states for us in the NEW Covenant that "**all things are lawful**" (**permitted**) however he reminds us to "NOT be brought under the **power** of any" of the above mentioned unrighteous acts...such as drinking too much. So it is not a question is it "forbidden"(unlawful) but it may be for us to simply decide that we will NOT be under the control or addicted to drinking to the point of intoxication.

Psalm 104:14-15 **¹⁴ He causeth** *the grass to grow for the cattle, and herb for the service of man: that he may bring forth food out of the earth;* **¹⁵** *And* **wine that maketh glad the heart of man,** *and oil to make his face to shine, and bread which strengtheneth man's heart.*

Here we read where the Lord causeth (makes) wine that makes glad a man's heart. So it says in this case wine can obviously be used for making our heart glad, maybe at a ceremony used to celebrate a special occasion, such as a wedding celebration.

Ecclesiastes 9:7 Go thy way, eat thy bread with joy, and **drink thy wine with a merry heart;** *for God now accepteth thy works.*

I believe here that even though it tells us to eat drink and be merry...we should consider where the man who wrote Ecclesiastes was in his walk. Solomon who wrote this book ends with the conclusion of "Fear God and keep His commandments, for this is the whole duty of man".

Romans 13:13 **¹³** *Let us* **walk honestly,** *as in the day;* **not in rioting and drunkenness**, *not in chambering and wantonness, not in strife and envying.*

Ephesians 5:18 [18] *And **be not drunk with wine**, wherein is excess; but be filled with the Spirit;*

We are reminded in these two verses to walk in honesty (integrity) and be filled with the spirit, verses drunkenness or excess, too much wine.

John 2:3-11 [3] *And when they wanted wine, the mother of Jesus saith unto him, They have no wine.* [4] *Jesus saith unto her, Woman, what have I to do with thee? mine hour is not yet come.* [5] *His mother saith unto the servants, Whatsoever he saith unto you, do it.* [6] *And there were set there six waterpots of stone, after the manner of the purifying of the Jews, containing two or three firkins apiece.* [7] *Jesus saith unto them, Fill the waterpots with water. And they filled them up to the brim.* [8] *And he saith unto them, Draw out now, and bear unto the governor of the feast. And they bare it.* [9] *When the ruler of the feast had tasted the water that was made wine, and knew not whence it was: (but the servants which drew the water knew;) the governor of the feast called the bridegroom,* [10] *And saith unto him, Every man at the beginning doth set forth good wine; and when men have well drunk, then that which is worse: **but thou hast kept the good wine until now.*** [11] *This beginning of miracles did Jesus in Cana of Galilee, and manifested forth his glory; and his disciples believed on him.*

Jesus turned the water to wine… his first miracle at a wedding. There are also some spiritual parallels in this story…however if Jesus completely wanted to forbid the drinking of wine why would he do this miracle? Yes it was "effervescent" … so it did contain alcohol.

I believe if you have an addiction to alcohol, it is probably wise to not drink at all. If you have a personal conviction about it… that would be a choice you need to make to abstain completely. I think for most Christians, this is the wisest choice they can make.

However, I don't see drinking a little wine that does not lead to intoxication being a sin or completely forbidden anywhere in the Bible.

My prayer is that we use wisdom, walk in holiness not conforming to the world, and be pleasing to God.

CHAPTER THIRTEEN

THE CHURCH, DISCIPLES, APOSTLES

Have we gotten it all wrong?

□ □ □

The church as defined by most "Christians" is a building that we go to on Sunday, maybe on Wednesday and other days for special events. It is where the believers come together in fellowship and worship. This gathering together of believers is so needed and helps to strengthen each other and help each other grow in our faith. It is also used an Evangelistic tool that unbelievers can come in to "hear" the Gospel of Jesus Christ, and be converted.

However, what does the word say "church" is? Let us take a look at the definition?

Jesus came to build his church on the rock of revelation that Peter spoke that "Jesus was the Christ".

In Matthew 16:18-20 we see the word Peter translated as Petros meaning small stone. We also see the word Rock translated as Petra meaning a rocky mountain or large stone. Some may also interpret this passage that the Foundation of the church is the revelation of God through His apostles and that Jesus is the Lord of the church, the cornerstone of that foundation. The Lord builds His church on the Truth, Himself.

I do not think it was God's intention to build His Church on the foundation of a simple human "man" which is fallible and can be unstable, as we see when Peter even deny's Christ, then goes back to his old lifestyle of fishing. Some may teach that Peter was the first Pope or Apostle that God would use to build his church. I know Peter was an amazing Apostle that God used to witness of Jesus and spread the good news that Jesus was the Christ, the Messiah which had come to save the world. He was instrumental in the book known as the Acts of the Apostles where they went into all the world to preach and teach this Gospel to new believers and unbelievers. The word apostle simply means "sent one", or one sent with a message. There were the twelve **Apostles of Jesus** that Jesus chose specifically from all other disciples to continue to spread the good news. They were eye witnesses of Jesus's resurrection, had been with Jesus to sit under His teachings, and were specifically called by Jesus himself. Then we see the "Apostles of the church" sent to preach the Gospel of Jesus Christ.

So what is "the church"? Most of us know by now that this word translates out to "ekklesia" in the Greek which means, "a calling out", "popular meeting of a body of people". So if here the church is NOT a BUILDING, but a gathering of people that are meeting together in fellowship, why is there SO much emphasis on "going to a building", "building funds", "building a huge edifice

112

with a steeple"? Well obviously if there are gatherings of people we will need a house or building to come together in to shelter us from rain or the elements. But I think too much emphasis has been put on "going to a building" rather than actually "gathering a body of people" which is the right context of the word.

We also read where Christ is the HEAD (the only AUTHORITY) over HIS BODY (the church). We see the word "Pastor" used only once in the New Testament, yet people have made it some high priestly calling or office, which it was never meant to be. Pastors are "shepherds" (poimen), not professional preachers or pulpiteers. They are called as a Shepherd or caretaker to "watch over and care for the sheep", to guard them and to even guard the "doctrine of the Apostles", "the Gospel of Jesus Christ", to make sure that the thief, the false teachers, hirelings, wolves in sheep's clothing do not come to lead them away from Jesus and His teachings. Bishops are simply overseers (episkopos), not high church officials that wear a miter of the fish god Dagon upon their head. Ministers are servants (diakonos), not official clergymen. Elders are wise old senior men (presbuteros), not ecclesiastical officers. We are discovering that the "leadership" terminology" of the New Testament tells us that these descriptions do not denote formal **offices**, titles or positions, but are "FUNCTIONS" in the church.

113

Romans 12:4 ⁴ For as we have many members in one body, and all members have not the same office:

This word "office" here in the Greek "*praxis*" translates out as "FUNCTION".

Let us look at the word "Apostle" used here…

1 Timothy 2:7 Whereunto I am ordained a preacher, and an apostle, (I speak the truth in Christ, and lie not;) a teacher of the Gentiles in faith and verity

The word "Apostle" here in the Greek "*apostolos*" translates out as "delegate", "ambassador of the Gospel", "commissioner of Christ", "messenger that is sent". Timothy and Titus were not pastors, but apostolic workers, who were sent from place to place – Timothy to Ephesus, Titus to Crete, to plant churches, strengthen and sort out problems even with doctrine or disorder in new church plants. Apostles break up the fallow ground and plant the seed (the Word of God) and lay the foundation of the church…so they are logically the first ones to show up on the scene.

We have Prophets who follow them next on the scene to progress the process and to supply the church with vision and give spiritual encouragements. Teachers then follow in their gift to build the church on a solid "doctrinal" foundation. Evangelists are preachers of the Gospel, and will plant the "seed" to reach unbelievers. Pastors then come to care-take, serve, guard and watch over the flock (the church body of believers). There is no

114

"greater" gift but a logical order of how things should be built given in 1 Corinthians 12:28. All have a specific function, but none are greater than any one function. Even the "laying on of hands in Acts 14:23 simply is an "apostolic public recognition" that confirms who the Holy Ghost has already called into a specific function and gifting, Acts 20:28.

*Acts 20:28 Take heed therefore unto yourselves, and to all the flock, over the which **the Holy Ghost hath made you overseers,** to feed the church of God, which he hath purchased with his own blood.*

We see in the New Testaments disciples of Jesus Christ. The word "disciple" translates out in the Greek *"mathetes"* which means "a learner" or "pupil".

Jesus did have disciples that followed Him, sat at His feet to learn the good news from the King directly. The King told them all about the Kingdom that will come, and what that looks like. Then Jesus demonstrated the power of the Kingdom with signs and wonders that confirmed who He was, in His deity, the Messiah, the King of Kings, and Lord of Lords. At that time He was the King of a Kingdom that was, is now and will be in the future. A Kingdom is the "rule and reign" of a King.

When Jesus Christ called His specific twelve Apostles out of His other disciples He gave them instructions that were JUST for them. These were the

Apostles of Jesus. If it were for all disciples, why wouldn't he have called them all?

So I believe we see in the four Gospels where Jesus Christ had called specifically His twelve apostles for His purpose and commission. In the Book of Acts, we see "sent ones", the **Apostles of the church**, that were called to go build a foundation for the "Way" and to continue to "Preach Christ" (the Apostles doctrine) to those different cities that had not heard or known of Jesus that were still in darkness. They were sent with this good news! Apostles never stayed and took up residence in a city for too long, as they were on a mission. They were NOT to build upon another man's foundation. We see in the Acts of the Apostles, that there was one specific Apostle, Paul, chosen BY Jesus himself, gifted and given a specific assignment to go to the Gentiles, where Peter was specifically sent to the Jews. Paul was an exception but again, as he had an encounter with Jesus on the road to Damascus in Acts 9:1-19. We see where there was a bright light and he heard the voice of Jesus that gave him specific instructions that he was to go hear these instructions from a man named Ananias, that told Paul in verse 15-16 the following…

*Acts 9: 15-16 15 But the Lord said unto him, Go thy way: for he is a **chosen vessel unto me**, to **bear my name before the Gentiles**, and kings, and the children of Israel:16 For I will shew him how great things he must suffer for my name's sake.*

116

We also read in Acts 9:9 that the men who were with him "heard the voice" (of Jesus). We also read in Acts 22:9 they "saw the light" (of Jesus) and were afraid. So there were people that actually heard and saw Paul's specific calling and commission come **from Jesus**. Paul was NOT "self-appointed", with NO WITNESS of his calling from Jesus.

Paul continues to give us an insight as to his specific calling as he brings his defense before Agrippa in Acts 26:1-23.

*Acts 26:15-18 [15] And I said, Who art thou, Lord? And he said, **I am Jesus** whom thou persecutest. [16] But rise, and stand upon thy feet: for I have appeared unto thee for this purpose, **to make thee a minister and a witness both of these things which thou hast seen, and of those things in the which I will appear unto thee;** [17] Delivering thee from the **people, and from the Gentiles, unto whom now I send thee,** [18] **To open their eyes, and to turn them from darkness to light, and from the power of Satan unto God, that they may receive forgiveness of sins, and inheritance among them which are sanctified by faith that is in me.**

We can take from these verses that a specific "apostolic" assignment is to be a witness of Jesus, and to go to minister to those that are pagans or lost to "open their eyes, and to turn them from darkness to light, and from the power of satan unto God, that they may receive forgiveness of sins". This is pretty self explanatory here.

Today's *modern day* "self appointed" Apostles are preaching and doing something entirely different. It is so disturbing to see self appointed "Apostles" preach anything else BUT Jesus Christ. In doing this, they have actually strayed from the Gospel, and are preaching "another gospel"

They instead preach signs, wonders and miracles and their goal is to usher in the Kingdom by the works of their hands that they do. They say they are to go to a seven mountain area of influence in our culture, to accomplish bringing the Kingdom of Heaven to Earth, by preaching revival, studying and following in the old revivalist's examples, manufacturing revival with man-made signs and wonders, so a great awakening and outpouring of the Holy Ghost will come. They are following men and their vain imaginations and not staying within the WORD of what Apostles of the church were told to do. We are seeing teachings such as mysticism, new age thought and pagan teachings come out of this movement.

Some of these churches are teaching their young people that they can go lay on the graves of the old revivalists to soak up their anointing from the dead. They encourage people to utilize Christian alignment (or aka tarot) cards or even prophetic UNO cards to prophesy to people. They encourage astral projection/travel by inducing it through prayer and meditation. It definitely teaches error…but can even move into heresy and pagan or occult practices.

Our **plumb line** for everything has to be **The Bible**. If we do NOT read about it, or see it in the Word of God, it is something that we should NEVER participate in. Getting outside of the Word of God is a dangerous place to be.

If there is only one important take away from this book, I implore you to PLEASE align everything you say and do with The Holy Bible in its full context. Study to show yourself approved UNTO GOD.

Read your Bible!!

CHAPTER FOURTEEN

LOVE

*What Does Christian Love Mean and
is it "Conditional"?*

□ □ □

We as Christians have a commandment to love God and love our neighbor as our self. This is not an easy mandate or commandment because we can all be unlovable at times. However, in 1 Corinthians 13 known as the "love chapter", we are given a warning that we can move in all the giftings given by God, but if we do not have love we "are nothing".

My questions are…are we to "love unconditionally"? Does God "love unconditionally"? Let us take a look at some verses to help us clarify these questions.

Matthew 5:43-48- *[43] Ye have heard that it hath been said, Thou shalt love thy neighbor, and hate thine enemy. [44] But I say unto you,* **Love your enemies**, **bless them** *that curse you,* **do good to them** *that hate you, and* **pray for them** *which despitefully use you, and persecute you;[45] That ye may be the children of your Father which is in heaven: for he maketh his sun to rise on the evil and on the good, and sendeth rain on the just and on the* *unjust.⁴⁶ For if ye love them which love you, what reward have ye? do not even the publicans the same?⁴⁷ And if ye salute your brethren only, what do ye more than others? do not even the publicans so?⁴⁸ Be ye therefore perfect, even as your Father which is in heaven is perfect.*

These verses spoken by Jesus give us a whole new goal in loving people. He tells us that anyone can love those that love back. But here He asks us to love our enemies, bless them, do good to them and pray for them. This can be one of the hardest things in our flesh to accomplish, as the "self" wants to preserve self, defend self, protect self. Self is the enemy of the cross. However, as we continue to practicing loving our enemies, we can move closer to being "perfected" in Christ as stated in verse 48.

*John 15:9-17 - ⁹ As the Father hath loved me, so have I loved you: **continue ye in my love.** ¹⁰ If ye keep my commandments, ye shall abide in my love; even as I have kept my Father's commandments, and abide in his love. ¹¹ These things have I spoken unto you, that my joy might remain in you, and that your joy might be full. ¹² This is my commandment, That ye love one another, as I have loved you. ¹³ Greater love hath no man than this, that a man lay down his life for his friends. ¹⁴ Ye are my friends, if ye do whatsoever I command you. ¹⁵ Henceforth I call you not servants; for the servant knoweth not what his lord doeth: but I have called you friends; for all things* *that I have heard of my Father I have made known unto you. ¹⁶ Ye have not chosen me, but I have chosen you, and ordained you, that ye should go and bring forth fruit, and that your fruit should remain: that whatsoever ye shall ask of the Father in my name, he may give it you. ¹⁷ These things I command you, that ye love one another.*

Here again Jesus is speaking and reminding us to continue in His love. He also states that IF we keep His commandments, we abide in His love. Then we see in verse 12 where He gives us a commandment to "love one another, as He has loved us". So I would say if Jesus is continuing to command us to LOVE one another this should be something we continue to walk in.

*Galatians 5: ²² But the fruit of the Spirit is **love**, joy, peace, longsuffering, gentleness, goodness, faith, ²³ Meekness, temperance: against such there is no law.*

Here we see a fruit of the Spirit is LOVE!

We also know that 1 Corinthians 13 is THE "Love" Chapter. I will post it here in the ESV Bible version, as the word "charity" is used to mean "love" in the KJV version.

*1 Corinthians 13:(1-13) **1** If I speak in the tongues of men and of angels, but **have not love**, I am a noisy gong or a clanging cymbal. ² And if I have prophetic powers, and understand all mysteries and all knowledge, and if I have all faith, so as to remove mountains, but **have not love, I am nothing.** ³ If I give away all I have, and if I* *deliver up my body to be burned,[a] but **have not love, I gain nothing.** [4] **Love is patient** and **kind;** love **does not envy** or boast; it **is not arrogant** [5] **or rude.** It **does not insist on its own way;** it **is not irritable or resentful;**[b] [6] it **does not rejoice** at **wrongdoing,** but rejoices with the truth. [7] **Love bears all things, believes all things, hopes all things, endures all things.** [8] **Love never ends.** As for prophecies, they will pass away; as for tongues, they will cease; as for knowledge, it will pass away. [9] For we know in part and we prophesy in part, [10] but when the perfect comes, the partial will pass away. [11] When I was a child, I spoke like a child, I thought like a child, I reasoned like a child. When I became a man, I gave up childish ways. [12] For now we see in a mirror dimly, but then face to face. Now I know in part; then I shall know fully, even as I have been fully known.[13] So now faith, hope, and love abide, these three; but the **greatest of these is love.***

So again we see where LOVE is admonished to be something we continue to walk in as a Christian believer and is highly valued.

A question arises when I hear others say we have to "love unconditionally". The love that comes to mind when I hear "unconditional love" is the love a parent has for their child. If we as parents, who absolutely love our children unconditionally, love them with a "co-dependent" love, is this a healthy love? Is our need to be "needed" and our fear of confrontation allowing us to love in an unhealthy manner? What does "self-less" healthy love look like? If we as a parent who oversees the health, safety and well-being of our children never "correct" or "warn them" of dangers in their path, is that real love? If we are afraid of rebuking our child and disciplining them when they do something that we know will hurt them, should we just NOT say anything?

I believe that a Father who truly loves his child will not choose what is "easiest" for him, but will choose to love in a way that produces what is, in the long run, best for his child. This is what I call self-less courageous love. Today we have parents that are practicing "permissive" parenting and allowing children to make even "unwise" choices for themselves when they do not have a fully formed brain (medically proven) in order to make wise choices.

In the same aspect, if we truly love others with a "self-less" love, should we do what is easy, or are we called sometimes to step out and love others courageously? This can mean that there have to be some boundaries and conditions set on the way we love people. Even our Father in Heaven gives us rules, discipline, chastening and boundaries because He loves us enough to not allow us to keep walking down a path that we make wrong choices that will inflict pain on ourselves.

*Revelation 3:19 [1]As many as I love, **I rebuke and chasten**: be zealous therefore, and repent.*

124

Here we see where God is speaking to the church of Laodicea that was lukewarm, the "apostate" church, and not really on fire for God and were a church in compromise. Here God promises those that He loves He rebukes and chastens! We also see this in many areas in the Word, even in John 15 where God will "purge" or prune the dead things from our lives that are not producing the "fruit" that He wishes for us to have.

So I say allow GOD to be our example of how to LOVE courageously.

Another question I have is, are we to LOVE our brothers and sisters at the expense of "sound doctrine"? Do we align ourselves in fellowship (and breaking of bread) of those that call themselves Christians that do NOT walk in "sound doctrine"? What about those that preach "another Gospel"? Let us see what the Bible says about it?

2 John 1:9-11 *⁹ Whosoever transgresseth, and **abideth not in the doctrine of Christ,** hath not God. He that abideth in the doctrine of Christ, he hath both the Father and the Son. ¹⁰ If there **come any unto you, and bring not this doctrine, receive him not into your house, neither bid him God speed:** ¹¹ For he that biddeth him God speed is partaker of his evil deeds.*

This is probably one of the most sobering passages in the Bible…given the fact that we hear so many now today in the Body of Christ saying that doctrine is not as important as loving people. True we are to love people… but look at what this passage says? THE WORD of GOD says… if anyone comes to you and doesn't bring "this doctrine" (the Gospel of Jesus Christ), that we aren't even supposed to RECEIVE him into our house. It also says that we are to not "bid him God Speed" which means to salute him or wish him well or pronounce a blessing on him, and that if we do this…WE are then a "partaker of his **evil** deeds". YIKES! Let that just sink in for a moment the next time that you wish to have fellowship with those that are preaching "another doctrine" contrary to the Gospel of Jesus Christ.

1 Timothy 6:3-5 *³ **If any man teach otherwise**, and consent not to wholesome words, even the **words of our Lord Jesus Christ, and to the doctrine** which is according to godliness; ⁴ He is proud, knowing nothing, but doting about questions and strifes of words, whereof cometh envy, strife, railings, evil surmisings, ⁵ Perverse disputings of men of corrupt minds, and destitute of the truth, supposing that gain is godliness: **from such withdraw thyself.***

We are told here, that if any man is teaching anything contrary to the words of JESUS and to the doctrine, that we are to **"withdraw ourselves"**. This is a pretty clear statement and instruction. I believe this is given to us so that we do not fall prey to deception and promote false teachings to others. If we even support or hang out with those that do this, this may create a stumbling block as

126

others may see our association as condoning these false teachings.

*2 Thessalonians 3:6 Now we command you, brethren, in the name of our Lord Jesus Christ, that ye **withdraw yourselves from every brother** that **walketh disorderly**, and **not after the tradition which he received of us**.*

*2 Thessalonians 3:¹⁴ And if **any man obey not our word** by this epistle, note that man, and **have no company with him**, that he may be ashamed. ¹⁵ Yet count him not as an enemy, **but admonish him as a brother**.*

Here we again are told to withdraw ourselves from brothers in the Faith that "walk disorderly" (to conduct oneself disorderly or immorally). We are also told in verse 14 that if ANY man does not obey the word, to have "no company with him", yet to gently admonish or warn him as a brother.

This is a pretty sobering thought, considering we don't see a lot of these scriptures talked about, as sometimes gently confronting our brethren in Christ is not always an easy thing to do.

1 Corinthians 5:9-13 ⁹ I wrote unto you in an epistle not to company with fornicators: ¹⁰ Yet not altogether with the fornicators of this world, or with the covetous, or extortioners, or with idolaters; for then must ye needs go out of the world. ¹¹ But now I have written unto you not to *keep company, **if any man that is called a brother** be a fornicator, or covetous, or an idolator, or a railer, or a drunkard, or an extortioner; **with such an one no not to eat.** [12] For what have I to do to judge them also that are without? do not ye judge them that are within? [13] But them that are without God judgeth. **Therefore put away from among yourselves that wicked person.***

Here again we see where Paul is bringing "correction" to the Corinthian church for immorality, and he advises us that we are to not judge those that are without (outside in the world), but to righteously judge the brethren within the church and if he chooses to not repent of his sin, as discussed in church discipline in Matthew 18, then we are to not have anything to do with him, UNTIL he is repentant. This is again what seems to be a very "unloving" thing to do, however, is it loving to allow our brothers in Christ to continue to walk in unrepentant sin? I would say no…it is cowardly not to risk confrontation for the goal of bringing a brother back to where he needs to be in his walk with the Lord.

*Romans 16:17 Now I beseech you, brethren, mark them which cause divisions and offences **contrary to the doctrine** which ye have learned; and **avoid them**.*

Here Paul is speaking to the brethren to "mark" them which cause division and offence by their false doctrine which is NOT a part of the doctrine of Christ. We do not see where unity is promoted here at the expense of truth or sound doctrine.

128

So we definitely see where there is a time to be separated from certain "brothers" in the church.

Galatians 1:8-9 *[8] But though we, or an angel from heaven, **preach any other gospel unto you than that which we have preached unto you, let him be accursed.** [9] As we said before, so say I now again, if any man preach **any other gospel** unto you than that ye have received, **let him be accursed.***

Here again we have a very serious and stern warning, and Paul takes it so seriously he repeats it twice, that if anyone even an angel from heaven comes to us to preach another gospel…let him be **accursed**. This is a warning for all of us that we are to "study to show ourselves approved unto God", be noble minded like the Bereans, and search the scriptures daily, and to stay in the TRUTH of what the Word of God says, and not to preach or listen to anything that goes outside of this truth.

Ephesians 5:(6-11) *[6] Let no man **deceive** you **with vain words:** for because of these things cometh the wrath of God upon the children of disobedience. [7] **Be not ye therefore partakers with them**. [8] For ye were sometimes darkness, but now are ye light in the Lord: walk as children of light: [9] (For the fruit of the Spirit is in all goodness and righteousness and truth;) [10] Proving what is acceptable unto the Lord. [11] And **have no fellowship** with the unfruitful works of darkness, **but rather reprove them.***

Here we are told to not allow any man to deceive us with vain (proud) words, because of what will come, the wrath of God, as it is disobedience to the Lord's commands. We are to NOT partake of that with them. We are to "prove" (test, examine scrutinize) what is acceptable to the Lord and to "reprove" (refute, correct) the works of darkness. So here I would say we have to speak out against these "vain words" and bad doctrine.

It is our duty as Pastors, Teachers and Leaders in the body of Christ to "guard" sound doctrine, as there are warnings in every book of the New Testament (except one) that warns against false teachers, false apostles and false prophets. We have to be a good leader and overseer in doing this in the Body of Christ.

CHAPTER FIFTEEN

CONFRONTING THE DEVIL

Should We Confront the Devil or
Satan Directly?

☐ ☐ ☐

How many times have we heard others Christians say, "I rebuke you satan". I have even been guilty of saying this myself and adding "in the name of Jesus" afterwards. I will never deny that there IS POWER in the NAME OF JESUS. However, when we do this "rebuking satan" all we have done is scold the devil. Let's take a look at some scriptures and see if we can determine whether we can confront satan directly.

Nowhere in the Bible are we told to "confront" or rebuke satan directly. We are told in...

*Colossians 3:17 And whatsoever ye do in word or deed, **do all in the name of the Lord Jesus**, giving thanks to God and the Father by him.*

The name of JESUS has the power to make free and deliver us from all evil...and JESUS is the only one who has ALL authority. JESUS is our "mediator" between us and God.

Matthew 28:18 *[18] And Jesus came and spake unto them, saying, **All power is given unto me** in heaven and in earth.*

In Matthew 28:16-20 we read when Jesus was speaking to JUST the eleven disciples (Apostles of Jesus) and he told them ALL power was given to Him, and to "Go teach all nations, baptizing them in the name of the Father, and of the Son, and of the Holy Ghost: Teaching them to observe all things". He never told them THEY have "ALL" power in heaven and earth.

Mark 16:15-18 *[15] And he said unto them, Go ye into all the world, and **preach the gospel** to every creature. [16] He that believeth and is baptized shall be saved; but he that believeth not shall be damned. [17] And these signs shall follow them that believe; **In my name shall they cast out devils;** they shall speak with new tongues; [18] They shall take up serpents; and if they drink any deadly thing, it shall not hurt them; they shall lay hands on the sick, and they shall recover.*

Again we see in Mark 16:14-18 Jesus appeared unto JUST the eleven (Apostles of Jesus) and gave them their "great commission" to go PREACH the GOSPEL to EVERY CREATURE. Then Jesus said for all that believe and is baptized, shall be SAVED! Jesus also said that "signs" will follow them that *believe*: They shall "cast out" devils...NEVER did Jesus tell them to rebuke satan directly or confront him or bring a railing accusation against him. He told them in His name to "cast out" or **command** the devils to leave the person, so that they are

132

healed and made whole. There is no special formula for "deliverance" method or procedure that Jesus gave us here. He never gave us a class on deliverance, he just said "in HIS name, cast or command them to come out".

*Luke 24:[46] And said unto them, Thus it is written, and thus it behooved Christ to suffer, and to rise from the dead the third day:[47] And that **repentance and remission of sins should be preached in his name** among all nations, beginning at Jerusalem.[48] And **ye are witnesses of these things.**[49] And, behold, I send the promise of my Father upon you: but tarry ye in the city of Jerusalem, until ye be endued with power from on high.*

Here again we see in Luke 24:33 Jesus found the eleven (Apostles of Jesus) and them that were with them. He spoke the words and opened their understanding of the scriptures and said to them, in verse 47 that "REPENTANCE" and "remission of sins" should be preached in HIS NAME among all nations, and that they were witnesses of those things. Then he gave them an instruction to go tarry until they were endued with POWER from on high. Remember, these are already followers and apostles of Jesus, but he wanted them to be "endued with power" (baptism of the Holy Ghost) in the upper room in the book of Acts.

Here again, we never hear Jesus tell his Apostles or disciples to GO confront or REBUKE satan directly.

133

*Jude 9 Yet **Michael the archangel**, when contending with the devil he disputed about the body of Moses, **durst not bring against him a railing accusation**, but said, The Lord rebuke thee.*

Here we see where Michael, an archangel, did not REBUKE satan directly, but said, "The Lord rebuke thee". In 2 Kings 19:35 an angel of the Lord struck down 185,000 in the camp of the Assyrians. Based on this we can see where true "angels of the Lord" have a lot of power. So, we can contend, while we are walking around in a flesh suite, a "corruptible" body, not an "angelic" body, that we should not confront satan directly, who is also a fallen angel.

*1 Peter 3:22 Who is gone into heaven, and is on the right hand of God; **angels and authorities and powers being made subject unto him**.*

Here we see where Jesus has angels and authorities and powers that have been made "subject unto Him"...not us.

*Colossians 2: ⁹ For **in him** dwelleth all the fulness of the Godhead bodily. ¹⁰ And **ye are complete in him**, which **is the head of all principality and power**:*

Because we are in HIM, Jesus, we are complete in HIM, as HE, JESUS, is the "HEAD of all principality and power". It does not say here that we are the Head. We can have direct access to HIM, who is seated in the heavens, as we are now given access by HIS blood, and we can ask HIM to intercede on our behalf.

1 Timothy 2:⁵ For there is one God, and one mediator between God and men, the man Christ Jesus;

Even when the Holy Ghost prays "through us" HE is still interceding for us...we do not have the ability to be the HEAD...there is only ONE HEAD...and Jesus is it!

*Philippians 2:⁹ Wherefore God also hath highly **exalted him**, and **given him** a **name** which is **above every name**:¹⁰ That at **the name of Jesus** every knee should bow, of things in heaven, and things in earth, and things under the earth;¹¹ And that every tongue should confess that Jesus Christ is Lord, to the glory of God the Father.*

There is ONLY ONE name...JESUS above all, with all power and authority, and it is not me!

CHAPTER SIXTEEN

AUTHORITY / HEAD OF CHRIST

The Pre-Eminence of Christ

☐ ☐ ☐

Who are we allowing to be first in our spiritual authority and our faith walk? Are we called as the Body of Christ to allow Jesus to be the "Head" over His body of believers? Or, are we allowing a man to be our spiritual authority even over Jesus Christ, the King of King and Lord of Lords?

Jesus is our High Priest, Our Savior and Lord, our Preeminence. What does preeminence mean?

The definition of **preeminence** is: the fact of **surpassing all others**; **superiority**: having paramount rank, dignity, or importance.

Colossians 1:13 Who hath delivered us from the power of darkness, and hath translated us into the kingdom of his dear Son: 14 In whom we have redemption through his blood, even the forgiveness of sins: 15 Who is the image of the invisible God, the firstborn of every creature: 16 For by him were all things created, that are in heaven, and that are in earth, visible and invisible, whether they be thrones, or dominions, or principalities, or powers: all things were created by him, and for him: [17] *And he is before all things, and by him all things consist.* [18] *And **he is the head of the body, the church**: who is the beginning, the firstborn from the dead; that in all things **he might have the preeminence**.* [19] *For it pleased the Father that in him should all fulness dwell;*

Here we are told that Jesus is the authority of His body, the church, and he should have the preeminence, NOT a man. However, there will be men that love to put their superiority and authority in the place that Jesus should hold. We see an example of this in the following verses with a man call Diotrophes.

3 John 9-11 [9] *I wrote unto the church: but **Diotrephes**, who **loveth to have the preeminence among them**, receiveth us not.* [10] *Wherefore, if I come, I will remember his deeds which he doeth, prating against us with malicious words: and not content therewith, neither doth he himself receive the brethren, and forbiddeth them that would, and casteth them out of the church.* [11] *Beloved, **follow not that which is evil**, but that which is good. He that doeth good is of God: but he that doeth evil hath not seen God.*

Here we see where this man loved to have the superiority over men. The pride that is in a man can forever be a hindrance to the humility that we are called to walk in as a servant leader. Man's thorn is that we are forever seeking after power...power to rule and control. We then see in these verses where it commends us to NOT follow that which is evil...man having preeminence over man, is evil.

Even Jesus warned us about man ruling over man in Matthew 20:20-28.

*Matthew 20:²⁰ Then came to him the mother of Zebedees children with her sons, worshipping him, and desiring a certain thing of him. ²¹ And he said unto her, What wilt thou? She saith unto him, **Grant that these my two sons may sit, the one on thy right hand, and the other on the left, in thy kingdom.** ²² But **Jesus answered** and said, Ye know not what ye ask. Are ye able to drink of the cup that I shall drink of, and to be baptized with the baptism that I am baptized with? They say unto him, We are able. ²³ And he saith unto them, Ye shall drink indeed of my cup, and be baptized with the baptism that I am baptized with: but **to sit on my right hand, and on my left, is not mine to give, but it shall be given to them for whom it is prepared of my Father.** ²⁴ And when the ten heard it, they were moved with indignation against the two brethren. ²⁵ But Jesus called them unto him, and said, Ye know that **the princes of the Gentiles exercise dominion over them, and they that are great exercise authority upon them.** ²⁶ But **it shall not be so among you:** but whosoever will be great among you, let him be your **minister;** ²⁷ And whosoever will be chief among you, let him be your **servant:** ²⁸ Even as the Son of man came not* *to be ministered unto, but to minister, and **to give his life a ransom for many.***

Here we see the mother of Zebedee's children, James and John (two apostles of Jesus) came to ask Jesus if her sons can have the "seats of power and authority" in His Kingdom. Jesus reminds her that it is NOT His to grant...but shall be given by His Father in heaven. He also then states a little reminder that the princes (rulers) of the Gentiles (world) like to exercise (have) dominion and authority over them (man), but states **"IT SHALL NOT be so AMONG YOU"**. So here Jesus is rebuking the desire to have a man rule over a man....and says this is not something we should seek after.

*Colossians 2:⁹ For in him dwelleth all the fulness of the Godhead bodily.¹⁰ And ye are complete in him, which is the **head of all principality and power***:

Here we see that "in him" JESUS dwelleth ALL the fullness of the Godhead bodily. JESUS is the HEAD of ALL principality and power.

*Ephesians 1:²⁰ Which he wrought in **Christ**, when he raised him from the dead, and **set him at his own right hand in the heavenly places**, ²¹ **Far above all** principality, and power, and might, and dominion, and **every name** that is named, not only **in this world**, but also **in that which is to come:** ²² And hath put all things under his feet, and **gave him to be the head** over all things to the*

139

*church, 23 Which is **his body**, the fulness of him that filleth all in all.*

So much in these verses which tells us that Christ is seated at the right hand (power) in heaven and is FAR above ALL…above every name in this world, and that world which is to come. He is the HEAD OVER ALL things to the CHURCH…HIS BODY. Why do we keep putting man in the place of Christ as the authority over the church? I believe even from Moses day, and the choosing of King Saul, that man still continues to keep choosing a man who they can see, although fallible, verses Jesus who they can't see, to rule over them.

We can look at some additional verses that give us a clearer understanding of Jesus' place among us.

*Hebrews 3:1-2 Wherefore, holy brethren, partakers of the heavenly calling, consider **the Apostle and High Priest of our profession, Christ Jesus;** 2 Who was faithful to him that appointed him, as also Moses was faithful in all his house.*

Jesus is our APOSTLE and HIGH PRIEST.

*Hebrews 6:20 Whither the **forerunner** is for us **entered**, even **Jesus**, made a **high priest for ever** after the order of Melchisedec.*

Jesus is our FORERUNNER and KING/PRIEST.

*Hebrews 4:14 Seeing then that we have a **great high priest**, that is passed into the heavens, Jesus the Son of God, let us hold fast our profession.*

Again we are reminded that Jesus is our GREAT HIGH PRIEST!

*Hebrews 2:17 Wherefore in all things it behoved him to be made like unto his brethren, that he might be a merciful and faithful **high priest** in things pertaining to God, to **make reconciliation for the sins of the people**.*

Jesus's purpose as the HIGH PRIEST is to make "eternal" reconciliation for the sins of the people. NO MAN can bring this redemption. No man will ever be able to deliver creation from the bondage of corruption...only JESUS!

*Hebrews 7:[26] For such an **high priest** became us, who is holy, harmless, **undefiled**, **separate from sinners**, and made higher than the heavens; [27] Who needeth not daily, as those high priests, **to offer up sacrifice**, first for his own sins, and then for the people's: for **this he did once, when he offered up himself**. [28] For the law maketh **men high priests which have infirmity**; but the word of the oath, which was since the law, maketh **the Son, who is consecrated for evermore**.*

141

JESUS was our undefiled, holy, sinless sacrifice that offered himself up ONCE forevermore for the sins of the people.

1 Timothy 2:5-6 [5] *For there is one God, and* **one mediator between God and men**, *the man* **Christ Jesus;** [6] *Who gave himself a ransom for all, to be testified in due time.*

There is only **one mediator** between God and men...CHRIST JESUS. We now have access to Jesus directly to go to Him to mediate on our behalf...we do not need a man to do that for us.

Jesus Christ is Our... Shepherd, Advocate, Mediator, Bridegroom, Conqueror, Lion, Lamb, Sacrifice, Manna, Rock, Living Water, Bread of Life, New Wine, Dwelling Place, Anchor, Wisdom, Peace, Comfort, Helper, Joy, Glory, Power, Strength, Wealth, Victory, Redemption, Profit, High Priest, Intercessor, Teacher, Kinsman Redeemer, Guide, Liberator, Prince, Deliverer, Captain, Vision, Beloved, Way, Truth, Life, Author, Finisher, Beginning, End, your all in all.

Jesus Christ is all of those things and more! Jesus is ALL we need.

We follow Christ, we proclaim Christ, and we simply...PREACH CHRIST!

CHAPTER SEVENTEEN

TITHING

It is Biblical...BUT Is It Christian?

☐ ☐ ☐

Is tithing biblical? This is an age old question. I will try and help bring some clarity on this issue; however I encourage you to study it out on your own and really dig into the Word, the history and depths of tithing.

The quick answer is YES tithing IS Biblical, but it is NOT a part of the NEW covenant for Christians. Before you scream..."you're wrong", let me just start by prefacing that we as Christians absolutely need to have the right "HEART" to give to all those that have a need whenever it is within our capability to do so. If you feel you want to support a church, or ministry, then YES, please give to that financially, especially if the Holy Spirit is prompting you to give...DO IT!!

However, NEVER give because you are threatened with a curse from the book of Malachi and never because you were emotionally manipulated by a public auction style giving to get the rewards or accolades from a man, and never give because you wanted to "GET" something from God. All of these are the wrong motives to give into God's Kingdom.

So let's dig into this a little and actually see what the Bible has to say on the subject.

The Lord called for three types of tithes for Israel in the old covenant and it was a part of their "taxation" system, what today would be known as a "welfare" system. The word tithe in Hebrew is "maser" which means a tenth. In the Greek the word is dekatoo also means to give a tenth. The "tithe" included the produce and seed of the land, the fruit of the land, and the herd. It was NOT MONEY.

Let us look at some of the scripture references for tithing.

The **first type** of tithe was given of the produce of the land and meat from the livestock to support the priests, the Levites, since they were not given any inheritance.

Numbers 18:21-31²¹ And, behold, I have given the children of Levi all the tenth in Israel for an inheritance, for their service which they serve, even the service of the tabernacle of the congregation. ²² Neither must the children of Israel henceforth come nigh the tabernacle of the congregation, lest they bear sin, and die. ²³ But the Levites shall do the service of the tabernacle of the congregation, and they shall bear their iniquity: it shall be a statute for ever throughout your generations, that

among the children of Israel they have no inheritance.
24 But the tithes of the children of Israel, which they offer
as an heave offering unto the LORD, I have given to the
Levites to inherit: therefore I have said unto them, Among
the children of Israel they shall have no inheritance.
25 And the LORD spake unto Moses, saying, 26 Thus speak
unto the Levites, and say unto them, When ye take of the
children of Israel the tithes which I have given you from
them for your inheritance, then ye shall offer up an heave
offering of it for the LORD, even a tenth part of the tithe.
27 And this your heave offering shall be reckoned unto
you, as though it were the corn of the threshingfloor, and
as the fulness of the winepress. 28 Thus ye also shall offer
an heave offering unto the LORD of all your tithes, which
ye receive of the children of Israel; and ye shall give
thereof the LORD'S heave offering to Aaron the priest.
29 Out of all your gifts ye shall offer every heave offering
of the LORD, of all the best thereof, even the hallowed part
thereof out of it. 30 Therefore thou shalt say unto them,
When ye have heaved the best thereof from it, then it shall
be counted unto the Levites as the increase of the
threshingfloor, and as the increase of the winepress.
31 And ye shall eat it in every place, ye and your
households: for it is your reward for your service in the
tabernacle of the congregation.

*Leviticus 27:30-33 30 And all the tithe of **the land**,*
*whether of the **seed of the land**, or of the **fruit** of the tree,*
is the LORD's: it is holy unto the LORD.31 And if a man will

*at all redeem ought of his tithes, he shall add thereto the fifth part thereof.*³² *And concerning the **tithe of the herd, or of the flock**, even of whatsoever passeth under the rod, the tenth shall be holy unto the* L*ORD.*³³ *He shall not search whether it be good or bad, neither shall he change it: and if he change it at all, then both it and the change thereof shall be holy; it shall not be redeemed.*

The **second type** of tithe that was given was again from the increase of the seed that the field brought every year. This tithe would be used for religious *festivals* in Jerusalem. If it was too far of a distance or the family couldn't carry it there, they could choose to convert it to money.

*Deuteronomy 14:22-27*²² *Thou shalt truly tithe all the increase of thy **seed**, that the field bringeth forth year by year.*²³ *And thou shalt eat before the* L*ORD thy God, in the place which he shall choose to place his name there, the tithe of thy corn, of thy wine, and of thine oil, and the firstlings of thy herds and of thy flocks; that thou mayest learn to fear the* L*ORD thy God always.*²⁴ *And if **the way be too long for thee, so that thou art not able to carry it**; or if the place be too far from thee, which the* L*ORD thy God shall choose to set his name there, when the* L*ORD thy God hath blessed thee:*²⁵ *Then shalt thou **turn it into money**, and bind up the money in thine hand, and shalt go unto the place which the* L*ORD thy God shall choose:*²⁶ *And thou shalt **bestow that money for whatsoever thy soul lusteth after**, for oxen, or for sheep, or for wine, or for strong drink, or for **whatsoever thy*** *soul desireth: and thou shalt eat there before the LORD thy God, and thou shalt rejoice, thou, and thine household,[27] And the **Levite** that is **within thy gates;** thou shalt not forsake him; for he hath no part nor inheritance with thee.*

The **third type** of tithe was from the produce of the land, however, this tithe was ONLY collected every third year and was used for the orphans, widows, strangers and for the local Levite priests.

*Deuteronomy 14:28-29 [28] At the **end of three years** thou shalt bring forth all the **tithe of thine increase** the same year, and shalt lay it up within thy gates:[29] And the **Levite**, (because he hath no part nor inheritance with thee,) and the **stranger**, and the **fatherless**, and the **widow**, which are **within thy gates**, shall come, and shall eat and be satisfied; that the LORD thy God may bless thee in all the work of thine hand which thou doest.*

*Deuteronomy 26:12-13[12] When thou hast made an end of tithing all the **tithes of thine increase the third year**, which is the year of tithing, and hast given it unto the **Levite**, the **stranger**, the **fatherless**, and the **widow**, that they may eat **within thy gates**, and be filled; [13] Then thou shalt say before the LORD thy God, I have brought away the hallowed things out of mine house, and also have given them unto the Levite, and unto the stranger, to the fatherless, and to the widow, according to all thy* *commandments which thou hast commanded me: I have not transgressed thy commandments, neither have I forgotten them.*

So we see in these three types of tithing, that it WAS Biblical. However if we do the math on these three types of tithing, that twenty percent was required yearly and 10 percent every three years. Add it up it comes out to 23.3 percent every year. So if God commanded all three tithes, why are we only asking others to pay ten percent yearly? Let us also note as I mentioned above that if we already have a modern day taxation system present in our nation that is being taken out of our paychecks to support those that are in need, why are we asking for Christians to abide by an old covenant requirement for the nation of Israel and use it to give to a new covenant church? Israel used the tithe for the support of their priests which had NO WAY to make money and received no inheritance of land to produce crops or herds. However, today, this is not the case. Also, it was used to support their Jewish festivals, which we do not have in a Christian church. But the biggest thing to consider is that when Jesus died on the Cross, a mediator of a better and NEW Covenant, that all the ceremonial codes and laws that belonged to the Jewish religion, were crucified and destroyed on the cross, and could never again be used against us. Thus, Christians in the New covenant never have to bring a blood sacrifice to the altar, or a heave offering, or any other "offering" as JESUS CHRIST was THE perfect sacrifice and offering, offered up only once for us all.

Colossians 2:13-17 [13] *And you, being dead in your sins and the uncircumcision of your flesh, hath he quickened together with him, having forgiven you all trespasses;* [14] ***Blotting out the handwriting of ordinances that was against us,*** *which was contrary to us, and took it out of the way,* ***nailing it to his cross;*** [15] *And having spoiled principalities and powers, he made a shew of them openly, triumphing over them in it.* [16] *Let no man therefore judge you in meat, or in drink, or in respect of an holyday, or of the new moon, or of the sabbath days:* [17] *Which are a shadow of things to come; but the body is of Christ.*

Tithing was a part of the Old Covenant and was a part of the Jewish law. The good news is that we are now under a New Covenant, and no longer bound under the religious laws and traditions of men.

Some argue that we see that Abram tithed to Melchizedek king of Salem in Genesis. Hebrews 7:4 confirms this. However we see where he tithed from the "spoils" of battle and not his own income/or herds. Abraham also only did this once in his life and he completely did this of his own accord, it was not a command.

Genesis 14:17-20 [17] *And the king of Sodom went out to meet him after his return from the slaughter of Chedorlaomer, and of the kings that were with him, at the valley of Shaveh, which is the king's dale. [18] And Melchizedek king of Salem brought forth bread and wine: and he was the priest of the most high God. [19] And he blessed him, and said, Blessed be Abram of the most high God, possessor of heaven and earth: [20] And blessed be the most high God, which hath delivered thine enemies into thy hand. And he gave him tithes of all.*

So if we are to use this example that we are to tithe to priests today, then we should ONLY tithe once in our lifetime and ONLY tithe from the spoils of battle?

So now we come to the most misquoted Book of the Bible. The Book of Malachi. Remember we are still in the Old Covenant under Mosaic Law. When God commanded that Israel tithe, and were to bring their tithes into the storehouse (used to store produce or as a food pantry) which was located in the Temple, it was to support and feed the poor, strangers, widows and priests.

First let us take a look at who was speaking to whom for what purpose in the beginning of the Book of Malachi.

Malachi 1:1 The burden of the word of the LORD to Israel by Malachi.[2] I have loved you, saith the LORD. Yet ye say, Wherein hast thou loved us? Was not Esau Jacob's brother? saith the LORD: yet I loved Jacob,[3] And I hated Esau, and laid his mountains and his heritage waste for the dragons of the wilderness.[4] Whereas Edom saith, We are impoverished, but we will return and build the desolate places; thus saith the LORD of hosts, They shall build, but I will throw down; and they shall call them, The

150

border of wickedness, and, The people against whom the LORD *hath indignation for ever.⁵ And your eyes shall see, and ye shall say, The* LORD *will be magnified from the border of Israel.⁶ A son honoureth his father, and a servant his master: if then I be a father, where is mine honour? and if I be a master, where is my fear? saith the* LORD *of hosts unto you,* **O priests, that despise my name.** *And ye say, Wherein have we despised thy name?⁷* **Ye offer polluted bread upon mine altar***; and ye say, Wherein have we polluted thee? In that ye say, The table of the* LORD *is contemptible.⁸ And if ye offer the blind for sacrifice, is it not evil? and if ye offer the lame and sick, is it not evil? offer it now unto thy governor; will he be pleased with thee, or accept thy person? saith the* LORD *of hosts.⁹ And now, I pray you, beseech God that he will be gracious unto us: this hath been by your means: will he regard your persons? saith the* LORD *of hosts.¹⁰ Who is there even among you that would shut the doors for nought? neither do ye kindle fire on mine altar for nought.* **I have no pleasure in you, saith the** LORD **of hosts, neither will I accept an offering at your hand.***¹¹ For from the rising of the sun even unto the going down of the same my name shall be great among the Gentiles; and in every place incense shall be offered unto my name, and a* **pure offering***: for my name shall be great among the heathen, saith the* LORD *of hosts.¹² But ye* **have profaned it***, in that ye say, The table of the* LORD *is polluted; and the fruit thereof, even his meat, is contemptible.¹³ Ye said also, Behold, what a weariness is*

151

*it! and ye have snuffed at it, saith the L*ORD *of hosts; and ye brought that which was torn, and the lame, and the sick; thus ye brought an offering: should I accept this of your hand? saith the L*ORD.*[14] But cursed be the deceiver, which hath in his flock a male, and voweth, and sacrificeth unto the L*ORD *a corrupt thing: for I am a great King, saith the L*ORD *of hosts, and my name is dreadful among the heathen.*

So we see in the first Chapter of Malachi that the Lord is rebuking the "PRIESTS" for the profane and polluted offering. It was the priest's responsibility and job to bring a holy "pure" offering unto the Lord. Let's continue to read on.

Malachi 2:[1]And now, **O ye priests, this commandment is for you.** *[2]* **If ye will not hear, and if ye will not lay it to heart, to give glory unto my name, saith the L**ORD **of hosts, I will even send a curse upon you, and I will curse your blessings**: *yea, I have cursed them already, because ye do not lay it to heart.[3] Behold, I will corrupt your seed, and spread dung upon your faces, even the dung of your solemn feasts; and one shall take you away with it.[4] And ye shall know that* **I have sent this commandment unto you, that my covenant might be with Levi,** *saith the L*ORD *of hosts.[5]* **My covenant was with him** *of life and peace; and I gave them to him for the fear wherewith he feared me, and was afraid before my name.[6] The law of truth was in his mouth, and iniquity was not found in his lips: he walked with me in peace and equity, and did turn many away from iniquity.[7] For* **the** *priest's lips should keep knowledge, and they should seek the law at his mouth:* for he is the messenger of the LORD of hosts.⁸ *But ye are departed out of the way; ye have caused many to stumble at the law; ye have corrupted the covenant of Levi, saith the LORD of hosts.*⁹ Therefore *have I also made you* contemptible and base before all the people, according as *ye have not kept my ways,* but have been partial in the law.¹⁰ Have we not all one father? hath not one God created us? why do we deal treacherously every man against his brother, by profaning the covenant of our fathers?¹¹ *Judah hath dealt treacherously, and an abomination is committed in Israel and in Jerusalem; for Judah hath profaned the holiness of the LORD which he loved, and hath married the daughter of a strange god.* ¹² The LORD will *cut off the man that doeth this,* the master and the scholar, out of the tabernacles of Jacob, and him that offereth an offering unto the LORD of hosts.¹³ And this have ye done again, covering the altar of the LORD with tears, with weeping, and with crying out, insomuch that he regardeth not the offering any more, or receiveth it with good will at your hand.¹⁴ Yet ye say, Wherefore? Because the LORD hath been witness between thee and the wife of thy youth, against whom thou hast dealt treacherously: yet is she thy companion, and the wife of thy covenant.¹⁵ And did not he make one? Yet had he the residue of the spirit. And wherefore one? That *he might seek a godly seed.* Therefore take heed to your spirit, and let none deal treacherously against the wife of his

153

youth. [16] *For the LORD, the God of Israel, saith that he hateth putting away: for one covereth violence with his garment, saith the LORD of hosts: therefore take heed to your spirit, that ye deal not treacherously.* [17] ***Ye have wearied the LORD with your words.*** *Yet ye say, Wherein have we wearied him?* ***When ye say, Every one that doeth evil is good in the sight of the LORD, and he delighteth in them; or, Where is the God of judgment?***

So there is a lot going on in Chapter Two. The very first verse tell us who God is speaking to and who He is disciplining. It says "O ye PRIESTS, this commandment is for YOU!" God was NOT speaking to the whole tribe of Israel here or the church, this was to the priests. God says to them, if they would not hear and lay it to their heart to give glory to His name, He would send a curse upon them and curse their blessings ...and then says he had done that already.

God also reminds them in verse four and five that he sent this commandment unto them that His covenant might be with Levi, and covenant would be of life and peace and He gave them to him for the fear they had for him and His name. He also goes on to talk about the responsibilities of the priests to turn others away from iniquity (lawlessness), and they should seek the law of the Lord. But instead they "corrupted the covenant of Levi" and caused many to stumble at the law because they did not keep His ways and have been "partial in the law". In verse 11 God rebukes Judah and says they hath profaned the holiness of the Lord by *intermarrying* with the daughter of a strange god. This could also mean they polluted the "seed of Levi" and that was another act of rebellion that was an abomination to the Lord. In verse seventeen we see where the sin of an insincere religious profession was rebuked by the Lord as they were saying that everyone that does evil is good in the sight of the Lord and he delights in them. They were compromising truth, and calling evil good.

So to sum up Chapter two...this REBUKE was strictly to the PRIESTS...who had caused the people to go astray!

*Malachi 3:1 Behold, **I will send my messenger, and he shall prepare the way before me**: and **the LORD**, whom ye seek, shall suddenly come to his temple, even the messenger of the covenant, whom ye delight in: behold, he shall come, saith the LORD of hosts.[2] But who may abide the day of his coming? and who shall stand when he appeareth? for **he is like a refiner's fire, and like fullers' soap:**[3] **And he shall sit as a refiner and purifier of silver: and he shall purify the sons of Levi**, and purge them as gold and silver, that they may offer unto the LORD an offering in righteousness.[4] Then shall the offering of Judah and Jerusalem be pleasant unto the LORD, as in the days of old, and as in former years.[5] And I will come near to you to judgment; and I will be a swift witness against the sorcerers, and against the adulterers, and against false swearers, and against those that oppress the hireling* *in his wages, the widow, and the fatherless, and that turn aside the stranger from his right, and fear not me, saith the LORD of hosts.*

In Malachi Three, the Lord predicts the coming of John the Baptist and Jesus who is a "refiner's fire, and that He would purify the sons of Levi that they may offer the Lord an offering in righteousness. In verse four, we see only then will the offering of Judah and Jerusalem be pleasant unto the Lord, as in the days of old.

Malachi 3: ⁶ For I am the LORD, I change not; therefore ye sons of Jacob are not consumed.⁷ Even from the days of your fathers ye are gone away from mine ordinances, and have not kept them. Return unto me, and I will return unto you, saith the LORD of hosts. But ye said, Wherein shall we return?⁸ Will a man rob God? Yet ye have robbed me. But ye say, Wherein have we robbed thee? In tithes and offerings.⁹ Ye are cursed with a curse: for ye have robbed me, even this whole nation.¹⁰ Bring ye all the tithes into the storehouse, that there may be meat in mine house, and prove me now herewith, saith the LORD of hosts, if I will not open you the windows of heaven, and pour you out a blessing, that there shall not be room enough to receive it.¹¹ And I will rebuke the devourer for your sakes, and he shall not destroy the fruits of your ground; neither shall your vine cast her fruit before the time in the field, saith the LORD of hosts.¹² And all nations shall call you blessed: for ye shall be a delightsome land, saith the LORD of hosts.

The Lord continues to speak to the PRIESTS in Malachi 3 verses 7-12 asking them to return unto Him and offer a "righteous" and holy offering, by not choosing to walk in disobedience to their Levitical Priesthood covenant and to offer the correct offering as commanded by the Lord for the proper sacrifice. It prompts them in verse seven to not continue to go astray from God's "ordinances". They "the Priests" were "cursed" because of their unrighteous disobedience to their covenant requirements, thereby bringing a curse upon the whole nation by their actions. This is about the "priests" lack of obedience to God, and them getting their heart right before they come to offer a sacrifice. God says if they do this then he will open up the windows of heaven and pour out a blessing. When the Priests are obedient, it will bring a blessing upon the nation as we see in verse twelve.

Malachi 3: [16] *Then they that feared the LORD spake often one to another: and the LORD hearkened, and heard it, and a* **book of remembrance** *was written before him for them that feared the LORD, and that thought upon his name.* [17] *And they shall be mine, saith the LORD of hosts, in that day when I make up my jewels; and I will spare them, as a man spareth his own son that serveth him.* [18] *Then shall ye return, and discern between the righteous and the wicked, between him that serveth God and him that serveth him not.*

In Malachi 3:16-18 God speaks about the faithful remnant and the Book of remembrance.

*Malachi 4:1For, behold, the day cometh, that shall burn as an oven; and all the proud, yea, and all that do wickedly, shall be stubble: and the day that cometh shall burn them up, saith the LORD of hosts, that it shall leave them neither root nor branch. ² But unto you that fear my name **shall the Sun of righteousness arise with healing in his wings;** and ye shall go forth, and grow up as calves of the stall. ³ And ye shall tread down the wicked; for they shall be ashes under the soles of your feet in the day that I shall do this, saith the LORD of hosts.⁴ Remember ye the law of Moses my servant, which I commanded unto him in Horeb for all Israel, with the statutes and judgments. ⁵ Behold, **I will send you Elijah the prophet before the coming of the great and dreadful day of the LORD:** ⁶ And he shall turn the heart of the fathers to the children, and the heart of the children to their fathers, lest I come and smite the earth with a curse.*

In Malachi 4:1-4 He talks about the Coming Day of the Lord and the return of Christ. He wraps up about the coming of Elijah the prophet in verses 5-6.

So as we can simply read what these Chapters say, it does NOT REBUKE the church people for not giving. The priests needed to obey and do their job in the Levitical priesthood, and not cause their people to stumble.

In today's New Covenant the Levitical system has been done away with, and JESUS CHRIST is our High Priest now!   Thank God we no longer have to burn sacrifices on the altar! Jesus was our perfect and ultimate sacrificial lamb! We are forgiven!

I suggest also studying some Christian History in the seventh and eighth centuries. Landlords in the European economy leased land and they used the tithe, or tenth to calculate payments. When the church started to own land across Europe the 10 percent went to the church instead of the Landlords. This is where the ecclesiastical leaders became landlords, and the tithe became a tax. The tithe eventually became a religious practice throughout Christianized Europe. I would be doing some digging on your own to get the full history on its evolution.

So I hope this will put into context a little more clarity on the subject of tithing.

My suggestion is to have a generous heart and to give to all those in need that you feel led to give to. Pour into ministries that the Lord leads you into supporting, and especially those that support widows, the orphans and those in need.

Acts 4:34-35 should be a model for all leaders and Pastors, that when the body gives to a church, the leader of that church is to distribute to all that have a need and there should be NO LACK! Have a heart to give, and love your neighbor as yourself!

CHAPTER EIGHTEEN

SALVATION

Are You Saved?

☐ ☐ ☐

This topic of salvation is greatly debated and discussed among great theologians. I will attempt to give some scriptures that I hope will bring clarity to the issue.

We see Jesus himself speaking to a Jew in John 3 named Nicodemus. He was coming to Jesus by night for fear the Jewish Pharisee's would see him. Jesus was pretty straight forward with Nicodemus and gave him some answers to salvation. Let us read...

*John 3:1 There was a man of the Pharisees, named Nicodemus, a ruler of the Jews: ² The same came to Jesus by night, and said unto him, Rabbi, we know that thou art a teacher come from God: for no man can do these miracles that thou doest, except God be with him. ³ **Jesus answered and said unto him, Verily, verily, I say unto thee, Except a man be born again, he cannot see the kingdom of God.** ⁴ Nicodemus saith unto him, How can a* *man be born when he is old? can he enter the second time into his mother's womb, and be born? ^{5} **Jesus answered, Verily, verily, I say unto thee, Except a man be born of water and of the Spirit, he cannot enter into the kingdom of God.** ^{6} That which is born of the flesh is flesh; and that which is born of the Spirit is spirit. ^{7} Marvel not that I said unto thee, **Ye must be born again.***

We see here where Jesus stressed that a rebirth must happen to enter into the Kingdom of God (the rule and reign of a King). Jesus goes on to expound on this…

*John 3:^{13} And no man hath ascended up to heaven, but he that came down from heaven, even the Son of man which is in heaven. ^{14} And as Moses lifted up the serpent in the wilderness, even so must the Son of man be lifted up: ^{15} That whosoever believeth in him should not perish, but have eternal life. ^{16} For God so loved the world, that he gave his only begotten Son, that whosoever believeth in him should not perish, but have everlasting life. ^{17} For God sent not his Son into the world to condemn the world; but that the world through him might be saved. ^{18} **He that believeth** on him is **not condemned**: but he that **believeth not is condemned already**, because he hath not believed in the name of the only begotten Son of God.*

We see again Jesus giving some additional instruction that NO MAN can ascend up to heaven, and the Son of man (himself) must be lifted up, and when we believe in Him (Jesus) we will not perish, but have eternal life. John 3:16 is one of the most popular scriptures ever quoted. Note that verse 18 says that he that **believes** is **not** condemned.

We jump over to John 6 and see that Jesus just performed a miracle and multiplied the lad's lunch to feed the multitude, a great company of people. He used the analogy of "bread" to teach them about salvation. Let us see here what he says...

John 6:²⁸ Then said they unto him, What shall we do, that we might work the works of God? ²⁹ Jesus answered and said unto them, This is the work of God, that ye believe on him whom he hath sent. ³⁰ They said therefore unto him, What sign shewest thou then, that we may see, and believe thee? what dost thou work? ³¹ Our fathers did eat manna in the desert; as it is written, He gave them bread from heaven to eat. ³² Then Jesus said unto them, Verily, verily, I say unto you, Moses gave you not that bread from heaven; but my Father giveth you the true bread from heaven. ³³ **For the bread of God is he which cometh down from heaven, and giveth life unto the world.** *³⁴ Then said they unto him, Lord, evermore give us this bread. ³⁵ And* **Jesus said unto them, I am the bread of life***: he that cometh to me shall never hunger; and he that* **believeth on me shall never thirst.** *³⁶ But I said unto you, That ye also have seen me, and believe not. ³⁷ All that the Father giveth me shall come to me; and him that cometh to me I will in no wise cast out. ³⁸ For I came down from heaven, not to do mine own will, but the will of* *him that sent me. [39] And this is the Father's will which hath sent me, that of all which he hath given me I should lose nothing, but should raise it up again at the last day. [40] And this is the will of him that sent me, that every one which seeth the Son, and believeth on him, may have everlasting life: and I will raise him up at the last day. [41] The Jews then murmured at him, because he said, I am the bread which came down from heaven.*

The Gospel or "good news" that Jesus was preaching and teaching was that He was their salvation, and that it was so simple...believe!

Let us look at some other verses that tell us about being saved.

*Ephesians 2: [8] For **by grace** are **ye saved through faith**; and that not of yourselves: **it is the gift of God**: [9] Not of works, lest any man should boast.*

Salvation is a FREE GIFT from God! You don't have to earn it!

In the following verses in Romans 10, we see Paul expounding upon the difference between the law (of Moses) verses the grace (of Christ). He also gives us a very simple instruction for salvation in verses 9-10.

*Romans 10:[4] For **Christ is the end of the law for righteousness to every one that believeth**. [5] For Moses describeth the righteousness which is of the law, That the man which doeth those things shall live by them. [6] But the righteousness which is of faith speaketh on this wise, Say*

164

*not in thine heart, Who shall ascend into heaven? (that is, to bring Christ down from above:) ⁷ Or, Who shall descend into the deep? (that is, to bring up Christ again from the dead.) ⁸ But what saith it? The word is nigh thee, even in thy mouth, and in thy heart: that is, the word of faith, which we preach; ⁹ **That if thou shalt confess with thy mouth the Lord Jesus, and shalt believe in thine heart that God hath raised him from the dead, thou shalt be saved.** ¹⁰ For with the heart man believeth unto righteousness; and with the mouth confession is made unto salvation.*

Pretty simple…confess, believe and BE SAVED!

We continue to read in Romans 10 the absolute necessity to hear Preachers of the Gospel of Jesus, as this is how faith to believe comes. Let us look…

*Romans 10:¹³ For whosoever shall call upon the name of the Lord shall be saved. ¹⁴ How then shall they call on him in whom they have not believed? and how shall they believe in him of whom they have not heard? and how shall they hear without a preacher? ¹⁵ And how shall they preach, except they be sent? as it is written, How beautiful are the feet of them that preach the gospel of peace, and bring glad tidings of good things! ¹⁶ But they have not all obeyed the gospel. For Esaias saith, Lord, who hath believed our report? ¹⁷ **So then faith cometh by hearing, and hearing by the word of God.***

In order to believe you first have to hear "the Gospel" preached. Let us take a look at a few scripture in the Acts of the Apostles.

In Acts 2:21 we see where we simply need to call upon the name of the Lord, but we can only call upon Jesus for salvation if we actually believe on Him first.

Acts 2: [21] And it shall come to pass, that whosoever shall call on the name of the Lord shall be saved.

In Acts 3 we see the first miracle where Peter and John were ministering there at the gate called Beautiful in the temple. Peter and John fastening their eyes upon a lame man, commanded him in the name of Jesus to rise up and walk, and he stood up leaping and walked, praising God. Then Peter preached Christ and advised them in verse 19 to Repent and be converted so their sins could be blotted out. Salvation starts with repentance!

*Acts 3:[19] **Repent** ye therefore, and **be converted, that your sins may be blotted out**, when the times of refreshing shall come from the presence of the Lord.*

We go on to read in Acts 4 where salvation is found in NO OTHER…but Jesus!

*Acts 4:[10] Be it known unto you all, and to all the people of Israel, that **by the name of Jesus Christ of Nazareth**, whom ye crucified, whom God raised from the dead, even by him doth this man stand here before you whole. [11] This is the stone which was set at nought of you builders, which is become the head of the corner.*

166

[12] Neither is there salvation in any other: for there is none other name under heaven given among men, whereby we must be saved.

We see in Acts 16 where Paul and Silas was in prison and they ministered to the Philippian jailer, and he asked Paul and Silas what must he do to be saved. They spoke the Word of the Lord. We then see that he and his whole house was saved.

*Acts 16:[30] And brought them out, and said, Sirs, what must I do to be saved? [31] And they said, **Believe on the Lord Jesus Christ, and thou shalt be saved, and thy house.** [32] And they spake unto him the word of the Lord, and to all that were in his house. [33] And he took them the same hour of the night, and washed their stripes; and was baptized, he and all his, straightway. [34] And when he had brought them into his house, he set meat before them, and rejoiced, believing in God with all his house.*

In Romans 5 we see where we, who were sinners, can be reconciled back to God through JESUS!

*Romans 5:[10] For if, when we were enemies, **we were reconciled to God by the death of his Son**, much more, **being reconciled, we shall be saved by his life.***

This is the most exciting GOOD NEWS ever!!!

SALVATION puts us back into right standing or being reconciled with God!

Let us not make this beautiful, sacrificial work on the CROSS about us...it is, and always will be about...JESUS!

CHAPTER NINETEEN

DECREEING AND DECLARING

Should we do it?

☐ ☐ ☐

I wanted to dig in to this teaching that is being spread around that we have the ability to "decree and declare" with our mouth that something is so, thereby causing it to manifest in the earth. So let us dig in.

First let us see what the definitions of these words mean:

Declaration = **a formal or explicit statement or announcement.** Hebrew word "nagid" means "commander", "caphar" means "to score with a mark as a record, to enumerate, recount"

Decree = **an official order issued by a legal authority, a king, that cannot be revoked.** Hebrew word "gazar" means "to cut down, destroy, exlude, decide", "choq" means an "appointment of time, commandment"

If we declare something we can say it as a statement of fact, to make something known, to recount it, to make a formal announcement. However, declarations are not "causative", which means just because I say it, does not mean it is true. Declaring intent is NOT the "active cause" that results in the effect of the intent coming to pass. The declaring doesn't "cause it to happen". Some say well, what about Romans 4:17?

*Romans 4: [17] (As it is written, I have made thee a father of many nations,) before him whom **he believed, even God, who** quickeneth the dead, and **calleth those things which be not as though they were.***

We have to read the whole verse in Romans 4 and we will see that Abraham **simply believed God**, who he **"even God"** calls those things which are not as though they were. Abraham trusted God. There are attributes that we will never have that only God has (omnipotent, omnipresent, omniscience). We are not God, and will never be able to "manifest" or create something by "saying it", GOD is the ONLY creator of ALL things.

*Romans 4:[3] For what saith the scripture? **Abraham believed God,** and it was counted unto him for righteousness.*

Our problem always goes back to "unbelief" and we have more faith in "self" than in God.

We also do not have the authority of a King to decree something as a commandment that is irrevocable, or to decide to cancel out or cut a command down, simply because we are NOT a King. ONLY a King can make a decree, give the authority to or re-issue a new decree that can override the old decree.

Let us look at an example in the Book of Ester where the King issued a decree, then reversed it.

*Ester 3:[12] Then were the **king's scribes** called on the thirteenth day of the first month, and there was **written** according to all that Haman had commanded unto the king's lieutenants, and to the governors that were over every province, and to the rulers of every people of every province according to the writing thereof, and to every people after their language; **in the name of king Ahasuerus was it written,** and **sealed with the king's ring.**[13] And the letters were sent by posts into all the king's provinces, to destroy, to kill, and to cause to perish, all Jews, both young and old, little children and women, in one day, even upon the thirteenth day of the twelfth month, which is the month Adar, and to take the spoil of them for a prey.[14] **The copy of the writing for a commandment** to be given in every province was published unto all people, that they should be ready against that day.[15] The posts went out, being hastened by the **king's commandment, and the decree** was given in Shushan the palace. And the king and Haman sat down to drink; but the city Shushan was perplexed.*

*Ester 9:[13] Then said Esther, **If it please the king**, let it be granted to the Jews which are in Shushan **to do to*** *morrow also according unto this day's decree,* and let Haman's ten sons be hanged upon the gallows.[14] *And the king commanded it so to be done: and the decree was given* at Shushan; and they hanged Haman's ten sons.

Unless the King specifically decrees it or reverses it, you do not have the authority to decree something.

Some will throw out Job 22:28 as a verse that says they can decree a thing and it shall happen or manifest.

However let us look at this verse...and who exactly was speaking to Job.

Job 22:1 Then **Eliphaz** *the Temanite* **answered** *and* **said...**

Job 22: [28] *Thou shalt also decree a thing, and it shall be established unto thee: and the light shall shine upon thy ways.*

If we continue to read through Job we will come to verse 42:7 to see what GOD says about Eliphaz?

Job 42:[7] And it was so, that after the LORD had spoken these words unto Job, **the LORD said to Eliphaz** *the Temanite, My wrath is kindled against thee, and against thy two friends:* **for ye have not spoken of me the thing that is right,** *as my servant Job hath.*

So we actually see where the Lord was calling what Eliphaz spoke "not right" to the point that the Lord's

172

wrath was "kindled against him and the other two friends".

Some also "misquote" Psalm 2:7 to say they have the power to "decree", however here we read where they are simply "declaring" what THE LORD "decreed".

*Psalm 2:⁷ **I will declare** the **decree: the LORD hath said** unto me, Thou art my Son; this day have I begotten thee.*

So again, as we read and study the Bible, we absolutely CANNOT take one verse out of context of not only the whole chapter, the whole book but the Bible as a whole!

Some will say, well didn't Jesus give us all authority in Luke 10:20?

*Luke 10: ¹⁶ **He that heareth you heareth me**; and he that despiseth you despiseth me; and he that despiseth me despiseth him that sent me.¹⁷ And **the seventy** returned again with joy, saying, Lord, even the devils are subject unto us through thy name.¹⁸ And he said unto them, I beheld Satan as lightning fall from heaven.¹⁹ Behold, **I give unto you power** to **tread on serpents and scorpions, and over all the power of the enemy**: and nothing shall by any means hurt you.²⁰ Notwithstanding in this rejoice not, that the spirits are subject unto you; but rather rejoice, because your names are written in heaven.*

173

NO, Jesus gave his 70 disciples only at that time (verse 17) the power over all the enemy (verse 19) for a specific purpose, and that was to confirm the Gospel they preached and to confirm Jesus as the Messiah, and nothing would hurt them. Jesus also reminded them to NOT get all proud in the authority He gave them but to just rejoice that their names are written in heaven (verse 20). We cannot keep taking a specific authority that Jesus only gave to a specific group, for a specific time with a specific purpose as an idea that it is for "all of us now" to do the same things they did then.

Some say that you have the same authority Jesus has. I would ask you to please read what Jesus himself here says in Matthew 28:18.

*Matthew 28: *[18]*And* **Jesus** *came and* **spake unto them***, saying,* **ALL power is given unto ME** *in heaven and in earth.*

If Jesus was going to give them all the authority that He had, as God manifested in the flesh, wouldn't He have said that?

So let's look at where this ideology of "decreeing and declaring" originated shall we?

The group or movement that makes such declarations claim that because we are created in the image of God, we, like God, can speak things into existence. No qualified theologian or Bible scholar will ever say or agree to this, as it is nowhere in scripture.

174

The idea that human words and even their thoughts can create or manifest one's future goes back to the "New Thought" movement, which began in the 19th century with an American mental healer named Phineas Quimby (1802-1866).

Religious historian Beryl Satter explains that the movement's leaders taught, first, that "the mental or spiritual world was the true reality, while the material world of daily life, the world of 'matter,' was merely a secondary creation of the mind." Second, they taught that "human beings had god-like powers. As God created the universe through pure thought, so on a lesser scale did people create their own worlds through their thought."

These "New Thought" teachers taught that your negative thoughts would creative "negative outcomes", where your "positive thoughts" create positive outcomes. This is to say that you can "create or manifest something by just thinking it"…or even speaking it out.

New Thought teachers like Charles and Myrtle Fillmore, who founded Unity Church in 1888, emphasized not only the power of thinking but the power of speaking as well, and claimed that by speaking "affirmations" a person could attain not only healing but also financial prosperity.

E.W. Kenyon, a Baptist pastor, incorporated "New Thought" teaching into his evangelistic healing ministry.

175

While Kenyon rejected the non-Christian principles of New Thought, he replaced them with his assumed so called "divine principles" and laws, that he believed Christ had granted to believers through his death and resurrection. He believed you could "manifest" your divine blessings by speaking it into existence and using scripture (out of context) to do so.

Kenneth Hagin, Sr., was influenced by Kenyon. Some regard Kenneth Hagin, Sr. as the father of the "Word of Faith" movement or prosperity gospel. This "prosperity gospel" was similar to New Thought philosophy, with its emphasis on positive thinking and speaking. The Word of Faith movement teaches that if Christians practice "speaking out or confessing" the Word of God they believe it will manifest in their lives.

Christians who "decree or declare" things over their lives today are, unfortunately, following the same line of thinking as New Thought and the Word of Faith movement.

The practice of "decreeing and declaring" things over one's life is, ultimately, an attempt to manipulate, or try and manifest something with their own will or words. In his book *Counterfeit Christianity*, Roger Olson explains that magic is "any technique for manipulating reality through paranormal means." In practicing "magic" is the same thing.

Prayer is bringing your requests to God and leaving them with God to decide what HIS WILL is in a specific situation in your life. YOU are not God.

There are sadly some Christians who do not think of their declarations as only prayers, but think they actually have *more power* than their prayers. One prominent prosperity preacher even explicitly asserts, "When you face a mountain, it's not enough to just pray…. You have to *speak* to your mountains."

This is simply NOT BIBLICAL.

If we have "faith" and "believe" that God's word is mighty and powerful, we believe in what He says and that it will come to pass. We have to simply TRUST GOD.

We also see that even when His Gospel is preached, it has the power, even unto salvation.

Romans 1:16 For I am not ashamed of the gospel of Christ: for it is the power of God unto salvation to every one that believeth; to the Jew first, and also to the Greek.

1 Corinthians 1: 18 For the preaching of the cross is to them that perish foolishness; but unto us which are saved it is the power of God.

We will also see where His word that goes out of HIS mouth accomplishes what He wants it to accomplish where He sends it.

Isaiah 55: ¹¹ So shall my word be that goeth forth out of my mouth: it shall not return unto me void, but it shall accomplish that which I please, and it shall prosper in the thing whereto I sent it.

We should simply pray to the one mediator between God and man, Jesus, and make our prayers and supplications known to Him, and trust and believe in His perfect will that will be accomplished in our lives.

*1 Timothy 2: ¹I exhort therefore, that, first of all, supplications, **prayers, intercessions, and giving of thanks, be made for all men;² For kings,** and for all that are in authority; that we may lead a quiet and peaceable life in all godliness and honesty.³ **For this is good and acceptable in the sight of God our Saviour;⁴ Who will have all men to be saved, and to come unto the knowledge of the truth.⁵ For there is one God, and one mediator between God and men, the man Christ Jesus;⁶** Who gave himself a ransom for all, to be testified in due time.⁷ Whereunto I am ordained a preacher, and an apostle, (I speak the truth in Christ, and lie not;) a teacher of the Gentiles in faith and verity.⁸ I will therefore that men pray every where, lifting up holy hands, without wrath and doubting.*

Simply believe that God's will be done and that Jesus Christ is your ONLY mediator!

CHAPTER TWENTY

CRAZY CHARISMANIA

What the what...?

□ □ □

There are so many different "teachings" and ideologies within the Body of Christ. One has to wonder how or why Christians can be SO divided on what they believe. We are warned in all the books of the New Testament (except one) to BEWARE of False Teachers, False Prophets and False Apostles...it should really not come as a surprise to us. The division in the body over what we believe has been around for a long time.

There are two specific movements that I see that are teaching in error...the "Word of Faith" movement and the "NAR/Hyper-Charismatic" movement. Again, don't be alarmed...we have been warned.

I know that there is one particular "teaching" that is circulating around the body of Christ about the "courtrooms of Heaven". I have watched some of it, and it is not Biblical. The teachers will take one or just a few verses out of context and twist them to say what THEY want it to say, instead of what it actually says. They have even inserted themselves into the place of authority that

ONLY JESUS CHRIST HOLDS. For those involved in this teaching, I actually pray for you and ask that GOD would open your "blind eyes and ears" to hear and see the TRUTH of the Gospel of Jesus Christ! It is so disturbing to me when you say that YOU, a man, have the power to deliver "creation from the corruption of bondage". YOU will NEVER have the power to do this...as you are NOT GOD.   Read the Bible...JESUS will in his second coming, return and set up HIS THRONE of David upon the earth. But YOU will not have this place of power that only JESUS holds!

Others teach "mysticism" in this movement and have actually written books on the subject. They are also the same ones that are teaching that you can go physically lay on graves to soak up the anointing from the ground of an old dead saint, or stick your head inside a wooden barrel to receive the anointing. They feel that it is perfectly ok to use "Christian Alignment Cards" which is the same practice as using "tarot cards" (but calling it "Christian"), to read or predict someone's future, or to prophesy to them. They teach that you can see people's energy or aura's and practice energy healing, and use dolphin therapy. They teach that you can pray and meditate to achieve "astral projection", which is simply a form of witchcraft.   They actually have teachers in their movement that teach this through a "Flight School". Their doctrine is so close to, if not the same as, New Age and Wicca/Witchcraft teachings.

They also have a ministry school where they feel they can "teach" everyone how to prophesy, and the prophecies have to be "all positive", no "doom and gloom". They also are against anyone that warns of the "negative to come", as this will not align with their teaching that they are setting up "dominion on earth now" …funny that the Bible speaks of "persecution" in the end time.

They do not preach "the Gospel of Jesus Christ", but instead preach "the gospel of signs, wonders and miracles". They say that Jesus was a man who is simply anointed by God, so that if He was a man, then that justifies them being able to do even "greater" (meaning "different" versus "greater quantity") miracles than Christ did. They view themselves as being equal to Christ…it is so disturbing. Their main focus is not pointing others to Jesus, but pointing them to "revival", and that this last great "awakening" (of 1-Billion people) will actually be what ushers in Jesus Christ's second coming. They actually believe they are sons of God having the same authority as Jesus, are being sent to the "seven-mountains" in the earth to take dominion and redeem creation from corruption, instead of what the Bible prophecies, that all this will be burnt up, and Jesus Christ will actually return with a New Jerusalem to set up HIS Kingdom on the earth. Jesus did usher in His Kingdom at his first coming, a Kingdom that was, is, and is to come.

I do believe that there are some people in this movement that really do believe in what they are teaching, which they say are "new revelations". I believe that "some" of them are truly honest, kind and loving people who truly love the Lord and have just believed the "ECHO" and lies of what their leaders (Apostles, Prophets and Teachers) are saying to them, and do not actually take the time to DIG DOWN into the Word of God for themselves to see if it is actually TRUTH. This movement actually goes against sound doctrine and theology, and "pooh-poohs" studying to show yourself approved unto God" by calling this legalistic. They actually value "fleshly experiential experiences" they say are from God over what the Word of God says. If you publically disagree with their teachings, they will piously label you as a "Pharisee". They manifest some unholy and even Hindu-like manifestations in their worship, but what is so much **more** concerning is they are teaching "pagan" and "worldly" doctrine verses what the Holy Bible teaches. We are all commanded to continue to "study to show ourselves approved unto God".

I believe we need to come into the unity of the faith, but not unity of the false, and not at the expense of truth. Universalism already promotes this type of coexistence.

My call for all of us in the body is to continue to pray that blind eyes and deaf ears and hardened hearts will be opened to the TRUE GOSPEL of Jesus Christ!

CHAPTER TWENTY-ONE

WHO ARE GOD'S CHILDREN?

*Does God Hate the Sin, But Love the
Sinner?*

□ □ □

There are so many catchy Christian phrases that just roll off our tongues, and again we repeat it, because we have heard it for so long, that we never really think to question it. But I commend all of us moving forward to actually start practicing the "pause" and align everything we hear with what the Bible actually says about what we are hearing echoed.

The argument from loving Christians I have heard is…"Aren't we ALL God's children?   And if we are God's children, just like you as a parent when your kid does something wrong, you still love them"? The second half of this statement is true…I still love my children even when they mess up…however, I am NOT GOD. HIS ways are not my ways and HIS thoughts are not my thoughts, and I will never begin to grasp "His Thoughts" with my itty-bitty "finite mind"…and please don't quote the scripture "we have the mind of Christ"…go study that one out on your own.

So I ask you ....does God hate the sin but love the sinner? Let's go to the Word.

First we have to realize who we are WITHOUT Christ's atonement.

1 John 1:⁸ If we say that we have no sin, we deceive ourselves, and the truth is not in us.

Sin is the core of who we are without Christ. Jesus came and became sin for us and stood in our place on the cross and took on the full wrath of God towards us the sinner...he took all of our horrific sin on Him...and pulverized it, and crucified it on the cross. God laid on Jesus the iniquity of us all, the perfect sacrifice and atonement for OUR SIN. Let us not forget the POWER of the CROSS...this is the whole foundation and basis for our faith!

We also see that GOD never changes, and He is holy and righteous and hates sin, it is enmity to Him.

*Psalm 5: ⁵ The foolish shall not stand in thy sight: thou **hatest all workers of iniquity**.⁶ Thou shalt **destroy them** that speak leasing: **the LORD will abhor** the bloody and **deceitful man**.*

We see here where it says He HATES all workers of iniquity (wickedness) and He will destroy them that speak leasing (lies, falsehood, deceptive things) and he abhors (loathes, detests) the deceitful (treacherous) man.

*Psalm 7: [11] God judgeth the righteous, and **God is angry with the wicked** every day.*

This verse pretty much says God is angry with the wicked. The problem with today's teaching of "God just loves everybody it doesn't matter what you believe" is they are not realizing WHO God is in all of his Holiness and Majesty. The teaching that "God's love is unconditional" is simply "not complete". The "fear of the Lord" has somehow left the church!

Hebrews 10: [31] It is a fearful thing to fall into the hands of the living God.

So how can God hate the sin and love the sinner? He actually doesn't just send the sin to hell he sends the sinner. However, He loves us enough to send His only son to obliterate sin which he hates and redeem us back to right standing with Him. He loves us when we are "made righteous" by the Blood of Jesus Christ. When Jesus saves us from sin…then we become His.

I pray for all of my family and friends… that they will stay attached to the Vine…JESUS. Without Jesus, we will never live the life God intended for us to live. There is only ONE mediator between God and Man, JESUS! This life… or the next… I have to hang on to my Savior!

I have experienced rejection after rejection… but **IN CHRIST**; I found **REDEMPTION!!**

About the Author

Linda was ordained and licensed with the IFJC- Louisiana Chapter in 2008. She is also the Founder/Executive Director/Mentor-Coach for Women of the Vine Ministries, Inc. since 2007. She is the Author of "Jilted to Jesus" published in 2020. She is a Certified Facilitator/Trainer and Louisiana Representative for Living Free Ministries Chattanooga, TN. She has held many positions in "official" ministry: Women's Director, Children's Pastor, and Youth Pastor, and Co-Pastor. Her desire is to see ALL women equipped, empowered and sent into their God-given calling, and see their dreams fulfilled. She dreams of a church, a BODY of CHRIST, that truly comes together in UNITY and allows the real move of the Holy Spirit. Her heart's passion is to point ALL back to Jesus Christ and preaches the simplicity of the gospel. She is an advocate for TRUTH and JUSTICE!

She was Kentucky born, Ohio raised, transplanted to California, moved to Texas, and ended up in Southern

Louisiana where she lives now. She is currently a business owner, realtor, and licensed contractor, teacher of the gospel, Jesus freak, Christian blogger, foodie, book junkie, nature lover, gypsy soul, tomboy, mother, wife, daughter, sister, friend, and servant at heart. She is not a fancy girlie-girl, and she prefers denim to lace, turquoise to diamonds, and boots to high heels. She is fiercely independent... to a fault, wildly passionate about justice and God, loves to drive NASCAR, ride motorcycles, and experience fine dining. Her story will rock you.

Please REGISTER on my Website/BLOG for updates and future books/teachings and events.

CONTACT INFORMATION/RESOURCES:

Website/BLOG: https://womenofvinela.com/

Instagram: https://www.instagram.com/womenofvinela/

Twitter: https://twitter.com/@linda_hudson

You Tube:https://www.youtube.com/channel/UCqTrf3ToI4-Fm6m4sTdfyJQ/featured